THE A B C

An " FEDD " type omnibus at work

LONDON:
IAN ALLAN LTD.
in connexion with
The Birmingham and Midland Motor Omnibus Co. Ltd.

Prototype of post-war Midland "Red" 56-seater omnibus, 200 of which are on order

THE RAPID GROWTH OF THE "MIDLAND RED"

IN this atomic age the sight of a clean-lined, modern omnibus is such a commonplace that one is apt to forget how rapid has been the development of motor transport—more rapid, in fact, than any other means of conveyance except the air. The 'bus traveller of to-day, comfortably ensconced in a well-upholstered, smooth-riding and silent titan of the road, will doubtless recall with difficulty that only twenty years ago he was bumping over cobble-stoned roads in a roaring, angular juggernaut whose solid tyres and noisy engine set up a relentless vibration which jarred every bone in his body—unless his nerves had been numbed by the icy blasts sweeping over the open upper deck to which he may have been condemned on wintry days. One wonders, too, whether the modern bus-driver recalls the bare driver's seat of yore, where the only protection against the weather was a tarpaulin sheet, and windscreens were unheard of.

The reader, then, may be amused to learn that the ungainly vehicle seen on page 15, the first motor-omnibus to run in Birmingham, was eventually abandoned as being "a little before its time." But that occurred within this century. For many years prior to 1912 the Midland "Red" Company operated horse buses in Birmingham, but in 1904 there appeared in the city this new type of road vehicle. For three years the new motorbuses were operated experimentally, being finally discarded ; not for five years yet was the Midland "Red" Company to become a motor omnibus undertaking.

On April 25th, 1912, the first motor 'bus to commence regular operation as a passenger-carrying vehicle in Birmingham arrived in the city from London. Two years later, however, the Birmingham Corporation acquired from the Company a number of the motor omnibuses then in operation and took over the whole of the Company's motor omnibus services within the city. From that time forward the company commenced to develop country routes radiating from Birmingham, the rapid and extensive growth of which has made Midland "Red" buses a common and welcome sight over so large a part of England and Wales.

The Birmingham & Midland Motor Omnibus Company Limited, more familiarly known as "The Midland 'Red'" now operates motor omnibuses over an area of the Midlands covering approximately 12,000 square miles with a route mileage totalling nearly 6,000. In all over 1,000 separate services are operated all over the Midland Counties, embodying Warwickshire, Worcestershire, Staffordshire, Shropshire, Herefordshire, Gloucestershire, Leicestershire, Nottinghamshire, Derbyshire, Rutland, Northamptonshire, Oxfordshire and Buckinghamshire. A certain number of stage carriage services operated by the Company run over the border into Wales. A complete list of the routes operated, with their route numbers, follows on page 5.

In addition, a number of Long Distance Services are operated by the Company between Birmingham and various larger towns and cities outside the Midlands area, including London, Manchester Weston-Super-Mare, Torquay and Paignton. Long Distance Services are also operated by the Midland "Red" Company between Leicester and Cleethorpes, Skegness, Mablethorpe and Hunstanton, between Worcester and Aberystwyth, and between Kidderminster and Aberystwyth.

The fleet of vehicles operated by the Company at the date of issue of this booklet consists of 1,467 vehicles, comprising 903 single-deck omnibuses, with seating capacities varying between 34 and 40; 489 double-deck omnibuses of both front and rear entrance types with seating capacities varying between 55 and 59; and 75 luxury type coaches for express and long distance Services. Full details of these vehicles appear later in this booklet.

As the section devoted to the Company's vehicles shows, the Company has designed and built its own vehicles since 1924, the engines and chassis being assembled and erected in the Company's own workshops in Birmingham. The bodies, also of the Company's own exclusive designs, have been built by body-building firms in various parts of the country.

ROUTES AND ROUTE NUMBERS

LONG DISTANCE SERVICES

ROUTES

Birmingham and Weston-Super-Mare via Gloucester
Birmingham and Llandudno via Wrexham.
Birmingham and Llandudno via Llangollen.
Birmingham and Bournemouth.
Birmingham and Manchester.
Birmingham and London via Daventry.
Birmingham and Llandudno via Ellesmere.
Birmingham and London via Aylesbury.
Birmingham and Great Yarmouth via Cambridge.
Derby, Birmingham, Cheltenham and Paignton.
Kidderminster and Aberystwyth.
Leicester, Skegness and Mablethorpe.
Leicester and Skegness via Spalding.
Leicester, Norwich and Great Yarmouth.
Leicester and Hunstanton.
Leicester and Cleethorpes.
London, Birmingham and Manchester.
Wolverhampton, Dudley, Kidderminster and Cheltenham.
Worcester and Blackpool.
Worcester and Aberystwyth.

"X" SERVICES

Service Number	ROUTE
X.25	Bearwood, West Bromwich and New Cross Hospital.
X.26	Wolverhampton, Stafford and Standon Hall Hospital.
X.27	Smethwick and Romsley Sanatorium.
X.34	Shrewsbury and Hereford via Orleton.
X.35	Shrewsbury and Hereford via Brimfield.
X.47	Coventry (Pool Meadow) and Exhall Lodge Hospital.
X.48	Coventry and Walsgrave Annexe Hospital.
X.62	Coventry and Market Harborough.
X.68	Birmingham, Coventry and Leicester.
X.69	Coventry and Leicester.
X.72	Birmingham and Gloucester.
X.73	Birmingham and Cheltenham.
X.74	Birmingham and Cheltenham via Pershore.
X.90	Coventry and Stratford via Blackhill.
X.91	Leicester and Hereford.
X.92	Birmingham and Llandrindod Wells.
X.93	Birmingham, Bridgnorth and Church Stretton.
X.94	Birmingham, Buildwas and Shrewsbury.
X.96	Northampton, Birmingham and Shrewsbury.
X.99	Birmingham and Nottingham via Sutton.

STAGE CARRIAGE SERVICES

Service Number	ROUTE
100	Birmingham, Sutton and Mere Green (New Inns).
101	Birmingham, Sutton and Streetly.
102	Birmingham, Sutton and Mere Green (Clarence Road).
103	Birmingham, Sutton, Mere Green and Roughley.
104	Birmingham and Cannock.
105	Birmingham and Sutton via Walmley (Anvil).
107	Birmingham and Sutton via New Oscott.
108	Birmingham and Sutton via Wylde Green.
109	Birmingham, Perry Barr and New Oscott.
110	Birmingham, Tamworth and No Man's Heath via Sutton.
112	Birmingham, Lichfield and Burton.
113	Birmingham, New Oscott, Parson and Clerk and Hardwick Arms.
115	Great Barr and Six Ways, Aston.
116	Birmingham, Kingsbury, Piccadilly and Wood End.
117	Birmingham, Curdworth and Hurley.
118	Birmingham and Walsall.
119	Birmingham and Great Barr.
120	Birmingham, Oldbury, Rounds Green and Dudley.
121	Birmingham and Langley via Londonderry.
122	Birmingham, Langley and Oldbury.
123	Birmingham, Causeway Green and Blackheath.
124	Birmingham, Warley, Bristnall Fields and Langley.
125	Birmingham and Wolverhampton.
127	Birmingham and Oldbury via Tat Bank.
128	Birmingham and Clent.
129	Bearwood and Clent.
130	Birmingham and Stourbridge.
132	Birmingham, Kidderminster and Bewdley.
133	Birmingham and Stourport.
135	Lye Cross and Brierley Hill.
136	Birmingham and Romsley.
137	Birmingham, Brierley Hill, Pensnett and Gornal Wood.
138	Cradley Heath, Brierley Hill, Pensnett and Gornal Wood.
139	Cradley Heath and Brierley Hill only.
140	Birmingham, Blackheath and Dudley.
142	Dudley and Bearwood.
143	Bromsgrove and Birmingham via Rednal.
144	Birmingham, Bromsgrove, Worcester and Malvern.
145	Birmingham and Bromsgrove via Barnt Green.
146	Birmingham and Rednal via West Heath.
147	Birmingham, Redditch, Crabbs Cross, Astwood Bank and New End.
148	Birmingham and Evesham.
149	Birmingham, Alcester Lanes End and Wythall.
150	Birmingham and Stratford.
151	Birmingham and Earlswood (Reservoir Hotel).
152	Birmingham, Solihull and Hampton Lane.
153	Birmingham and Monkspath (George and Dragon).
154	Birmingham, Monkspath and Solihull via Blossomfield.
155	Birmingham and Knowle.
156	Birmingham and Chadwick End.
157	Birmingham and Leamington via Main Road.
158	Birmingham, Hampton-in-Arden and Coventry.
159	Birmingham and Coventry via Meriden.
161	Birmingham, Castle Bromwich and Coleshill via Water Orton.
162	Birmingham, Coleshill, Nuneaton and Leicester.
163	Birmingham and Castle Bromwich.
164	Birmingham and Leamington via Rowington.
165	Birmingham, Marston Green and Coleshill.
166	Birmingham and Marston Green.

Service Number	ROUTE
168	Birmingham, Castle Bromwich and Coleshill via Bacon's End.
169	Birmingham and Bacon's End.
171	Birmingham and Water Orton.
172	Wythall and Acocks Green.
173	Acocks Green and Yardley via Lyndon Road.
174	Acocks Green and Sheldon via Ideal Estate.
175	Solihull and Marston Green.
177	Leamington, Honiley (Boot Inn) and Knowle.
178	Birmingham and Earlswood via Tidbury Green.
179	Birmingham and Earlswood via Church Road and Tidbury Green.
180	Birmingham and Tanworth in Arden.
181	Birmingham and Monkspath (Cranmore Boulevard).
182	Birmingham and Kinver.
183	Birmingham and Shirley (Stanway Road).
184	Birmingham and Elmdon Heath.
185	Birmingham and Solihull via Streetsbrook Road.
186	Birmingham and Barston.
187	Birmingham, Solihull and Bentley Heath.
188	Birmingham and Beeches Estate.
189	Six Ways and Beeches Estate.
190	Birmingham, Stourbridge and Bridgnorth.
191	Birmingham, Kidderminster and Tenbury Wells.
192	Birmingham, Kidderminster, Cleobury, Hopton Wafers, Clee Hill and Ludlow.
193	Birmingham and Church Stretton.
194	Birmingham and Worcester via Hagley.
195	Birmingham, Wolverhampton and Stafford.
198	Birmingham and Tamworth via Curdworth.
199	Handsworth, Smethwick, Warley, Halesowen and Clent.
200	Smethwick, Warley and Quinton.
202	Cradley Heath, Blackheath and Round Hills Estate via Barrs Road.
204	Bearwood, Warley and West Smethwick.
206	Halesowen (Cornbow), Romsley and Manchester Inn.
207	Birmingham, Bearwood, Howley Grange and Halesowen.
208	Birmingham, Bearwood and Woodgate via Howley Grange.
209	Woodgate and Halesowen.
210	Handsworth, Smethwick and Oldbury.
211	Dudley and Swindon.
212	Londonderry Circular.
213	Bearwood, Windmill Lane and Handsworth.
214	Warley, Cape Hill and Londonderry.
215	Bearwood, Smethwick, Langley and Oldbury.
217	Halesowen and Oldbury.
218	Oldbury and Blackheath.
219	Oldbury, Grace Mary Estate and Oakham.
220	Bearwood (Adkins Lane), Smethwick and West Bromwich (Dartmouth Square).
221	Bearwood, West Smethwick and West Bromwich.
223	Warley, Londonderry, Smethwick and Avery's Works.
224	Bearwood and Warley.
225	Cradley Heath and Hayley Green via Old Hill.
226	Halesowen and Dudley via Old Hill.
227	Dudley and Oldbury via Portway.
228	Lye Cross and Dudley via Saltwells.
230	Dudley and Blackheath via Old Hill.
231	Cradley Heath and Blackheath via Old Hill.
232	Blackheath and Old Hill.
233	Bearwood, Warley, Causeway Green and Oldbury.
234	Causeway Green Hostel and Dartmouth Road.
235	Stourbridge, Lye Cross, Brierley Hill and Wordsley Green.

Service Number	ROUTE
237	Cradley Heath, Brierley Hill and Bromley.
239	Stourbridge and Cradley Heath via Quarry Bank.
240	Stourbridge and Cradley Heath via Overend.
241	Stourbridge and Cradley Heath via Cradley.
242	Cradley Heath and Dudley.
244	Dudley and Wednesbury via Locarno Estate and Great Bridge.
245	Stourbridge, Dudley and Wednesbury.
246	Stourbridge, Brierley Hill and Dudley Station.
247	Dudley Station, Princes End and Wednesbury.
248	Stourbridge, Dudley, Tipton and Princes End.
249	Stourbridge and Enville.
250	Stourbridge and Kinver.
251	Bilston and Coseley (Horse and Jockey).
254	Stourbridge, Enville and Bridgnorth.
255	Stourbridge, Bobbington and Halfpenny Green.
256	Stourbridge and Wolverhampton via Mount Pleasant, Kingswinford and Wallheath.
257	Stourbridge and Kingswinford.
260	Dudley and Kingswinford.
261	Dudley and Wall Heath.
264	Dudley and Coombs Wood via Old Hill.
267	Sedgley, Deepfields Station and Moor Street.
269	Dudley and Brierley Hill.
270	Dudley and Bilston via Princes End.
271	Dudley, Roseville and Bilston.
272	Sedgley, Tipton and Great Bridge.
273	Sedgley, Bilston and Wednesbury.
274	Sedgley and James Bridge.
275	Sedgley, Wednesbury and Myvod Estate.
276	Sedgley, Wednesbury and Darlaston Green.
277	Willenhall and Darlaston.
278	Wednesbury, Dudley and Prestwood Sanatorium.
279	Hurst Hill and Bilston via Ladymoor.
280	Hurst Hill and Bilston via Roseville.
282	Brierley Hill and Hawbush Road.
285	Wednesbury, Dudley and Kinver.
286	Dudley and Kinver.
288	Ludlow and Cleobury Mortimer.
289	Ludlow, Clee Hill and Hopton Bank.
290	Kidderminster, Hopton Wafers and Clee Hill.
291	Kidderminster, Newnham Bridge and Tenbury Wells.
292	Kidderminster, Bliss Gate, Far Forest and Cleobury Mortimer.
293	Kidderminster and Far Forest.
294	Kidderminster and Heightington.
295	Kidderminster, Rock Cross and Mamble.
296	Kidderminster and Alveley.
297	Kidderminser Arley and Bridgnorth.
298	Kidderminster and Arley.
299	Kidderminster and Wolverley.
300	Kidderminster, Wolverley and Lower Kingsford and Upper Kingsford.
301	Kidderminster, Shrawley, Stanford Bridge and Stockton.
302	Kidderminster and Ombersley via Stourport and Crossway Green.
303	Kidderminster, Stourport, Pensax, Menithwood and Clows Top.
304	Kidderminster and Kinver.
305	Worcester, Sinton Green and Wichenford.
306	Worcester, Wichenford and Ockeridge Cross Roads.
307	Worcester and Shelsey Kings.
308	Worcester and Stockton on Teme.
309	Kidderminster, Chaddesley and Elmbridge.
310	Worcester and Menith Wood.

Service Number	ROUTE
311	Kidderminster and Stourbridge via Hagley.
312	Stourport, Shrawley and Worcester.
313	Kidderminster and Astley via Wilden.
314	Kidderminster, Wilden and Hartlebury.
315	Stourbridge, Kidderminster and Worcester via Hagley.
316	Stourbridge, Kidderminster and Worcester via Norton.
317	Kidderminster and Bromsgrove via Chaddesley.
318	Bromsgrove and Stourbridge via Belbroughton.
321	Kidderminster and Clent.
322	Bromsgrove and Redditch via Hewell.
323	Sidemoor, Bromsgrove Town and Railway Station.
324	Bromsgrove and Lower Bentley.
325	Bromsgrove, Stoke Works and Droitwich Spa.
326	Bromsgrove and Worcester via Hanbury.
327	Bromsgrove, Hanbury and Feckenham.
328	Bromsgrove and Bournheath.
329	Upper Catshill and Bromsgrove Station.
330	Bromsgrove and Rednal via Barnt Green.
331	Bromsgrove and Rednal via Lickey.
332	Bromsgrove and Longbridge.
334	Bromsgrove and Dodford.
335	Bromsgrove, Manchester Inn and Romsley.
336	Kidderminster and Bromsgrove via Drayton.
337	Droitwich and Elmley Lovett.
338	Stanklyn Lane Hostel and Elmley Lovett.
339	Bromsgrove, Redditch and Stratford via Studley, Alcester and Haselor
342	Redditch and Evesham via Dunnington Cross Roads.
343	Birmingham and Redditch via Wythall and Beoley.
346	Ombersley and Elmley Lovett Aerodrome.
347	Astwood Bank and Triplex Works (Kings Norton).
349	Droitwich and Holt Fleet.
350	Worcester and Upton Snodsbury.
351	Redditch, Inkberrow and Worcester.
352	Droitwich and Kidderminster.
354	Worcester, Holt Heath and Holt Fleet.
355	Worcester, Crowle, Himbleton and Stock Green.
356	Worcester and Peopleton.
357	Worcester and Croome.
358	Worcester, Kempsey and Upton-on-Severn.
359	Worcester and Kempsey.
360	Worcester and Naunton Beauchamp.
361	Worcester, Hanley Swan, Welland and Rye Cross.
362	Worcester and Old Hills via Callow End.
363	Worcester and Malvern Wells via Welland.
364	Gt. Malvern and Tewkesbury.
365	Worcester and High House.
366	Worcester, Clifton, The Shelsleys and Tenbury Broad Heath.
367	Worcester and Clifton-on-Teme.
368	Worcester, Berrow Green and Ankerdine.
370	Worcester and Broadheath.
371	Cradley and Bromyard.
372	Worcester, Suckley, Acton Green and Bromyard.
373	Worcester Leigh Court, Alfrick and Longley Green.
374	Gt. Malvern, Upon-on-Severn and Evesham.
376	Cradley and Gt. Malvern via Leigh Sinton.
377	Cradley and Gt. Malvern via Mathon.
378	Worcester and Barnards Green (TRE) via Malvern Link.
380	Worcester and Poolbrook via Madresfield.
381	Pershore and Birlingham.
383	Pershore Town and Railway Station.

Routes 385-447

Service Number	ROUTE
385	Worcester, Pershore, Elmley Castle and Evesham.
386	Worcester and Pershore.
387	Worcester and Evesham.
388	Evesham, Cropthorne and Pershore.
389	Evesham, Broadway and Willersey.
390	Evesham Circular via Wickhamford.
391	Evesham, Badsey and Bretforton.
392	Evesham, Chipping Campden and Moreton-in-the-Marsh.
393	Evesham and Broad Campden.
394	Evesham, Offenham Circular.
395	Evesham, Offenham and South Littleton (Chapel Lane), or Cleeve Prior.
396	Evesham and Winchcombe.
397	Evesham and Pebworth.
398	Evesham and North Littleton via Badsey Oak.
399	Evesham, Broadway and Stanton via Childswickham.
400	Evesham, Broadway and Snowshill.
401	Evesham, Elmley Castle and The Cambertons (via Cropthorne).
402	Evesham and Bishampton Circular.
403	Evesham, The Lenches, Radford and Abbotts Morton.
404	Evesham and Pershore via Netherton Turn.
405	Evesham, Fladbury, Lower Moor and Pershore.
406	Evesham, Lenchwick and Norton.
407	Radford and Alcester Grammar School.
408	Evesham and Childswickham Circular.
409	Hereford and Birmingham.
410	Worcester and Orleton via Martley, Shelsley and Stanford.
411	Worcester and Fromes Hill.
412	Fromes Hill and Hereford.
413	Birmingham, Ross-on-Wye and Whitchurch.
414	Worcester and Ludlow.
415	Bromyard and Hereford via Pencombe and Ullingswick
416	Hereford and Tarrington.
417	Hereford, Ledbury and Worcester.
418	Ledbury, Colwall and Mathon.
419	Cradley and Ledbury via Coddington Turn.
420	Hereford, Bromyard and Worcester.
421	Worcester and Whitbourne Schools.
422	Bromyard and Docklow.
423	Hereford and Leominster via England's Gate.
424	Hereford and Leominster via Bishops Frome.
425	Hereford, Marden and Litmarsh.
426	Hereford and Marden.
427	Worcester, Clifton, Tedstone and Bromyard.
428	Hereford and Bodenham.
429	Hereford and Risbury.
430	Hereford, Burley Gate and Much Cowarne.
431	Leominster and Stoke Prior.
432	Hereford and Leominster via Dinmore Hill.
433	Hereford, Leominster and Presteign.
434	Leominster and Presteign.
435	Leominster and Puddleston.
436	Leominster and Hatfield.
437	Hereford and Leominster via Bodenham.
438	Hereford and Wellington Village.
439	Hereford, Tillington and Wormsley.
440	Hereford, Eardisley and Hay.
441	Hereford, Swainshill and Staunton Cross Roads.
445	Hereford and Almeley Sanatorium.
446	Hereford and Eardisley.
447	Hereford and Staunton Cross Roads.

Service Number	ROUTE
448	Hereford and Madley.
449	Hereford, Madley and Bredwardine.
451	Hereford and Thruxton.
452	Hereford, Withington, Westhide and Whitestones.
454	Hereford and Holme Lacy.
459	Hereford and Newtown.
461	Ross and Linton.
462	Hereford, Ashperton, Little Marcle and Ledbury.
463	Hereford, Bredwardine and Hay.
464	Hay, Clyro, Rhydspence and Brilley.
465	Hereford and Frome.
466	Hereford and Fownhope.
467	Hereford and Woolhope.
468	Hereford and Ross via Fownhope and Gatsford.
469	Hereford, Bishops Frome and Bromyard.
470	Bishops Frome and Bromyard.
471	Ross and Brampton Abbotts.
472	Ross and Ledbury via Main Road.
474	Ledbury and Wellington Heath.
475	Ross and Ledbury via Yatton.
476	Ledbury, Rushall and Kynaston.
477	Hereford, Ledbury and Gt. Malvern.
478	Hereford, Fownhope and Ross.
479	Hereford and Ledbury via Kynaston.
480	Banbury and Shipston via Upper Brailes.
481	Banbury and Shipston via Cherington.
482	Banbury and Sibford Ferris.
486	Banbury and Bloxham.
487	Banbury and Hook Norton.
488	Banbury and Chipping Norton via Main Road.
489	Banbury and Long Compton.
490	Banbury and Adderbury West.
491	Banbury, Adderbury and Deddington.
492	Banbury, Croughton and Buckingham.
493	Banbury, Adderbury and Milton.
494	Banbury, Brackley and Buckingham.
496	Banbury and Chipping Camden.
497	Banbury and Chipping Norton via Hook Norton.
498	Banbury and Burford.
499	Banbury and Charlton.
500	Banbury, Middleton Cheney and Brackley
501	Banbury and Middleton Cheney.
503	Banbury and Upper Boddington.
505	Banbury and Edge Hills.
506	Banbury Hempton and Nether Worton.
507	Banbury and Leamington via Ladbroke.
508	Banbury, Middleton Cheney and Greatworth.
509	Coventry and Banbury via Southam.
510	Banbury, Bloxham and Hempton.
511	Banbury and Rugby via Daventry.
512	Banbury, Brackley, Silverstone and Northampton.
513	Banbury and Mollington.
514	Banbury, Cropredy and Claydon.
515	Leamington and Banbury via Prior Marston.
516	Banbury, Lower Boddington and Byfield.
517	Leamington and Coventry via Kenilworth (Clock).
518	Coventry and Stratford via Leamington.
519	Stratford and Shipston.
524	Evesham, Broadway and Stratford.
529	Banbury and North End.

Routes 530-598

Service Number	ROUTE
530	Banbury and Tysoe via Shenington.
531	Banbury and Wroxton.
532	Banbury, Epwell and Shenington.
534	Shipston and Banbury via Epwell.
535	Banbury and Epwell.
536	Leamington and Coventry via Kenilworth and Windy Arbour.
537	Kenilworth and Burton Green.
538	Leamington and Kenilworth via Dalehouse Lane.
542	Coventry and Alcester (Hospital). (First Sunday in the month.)
544	Leamington, Warwick and Hatton.
546	Leamington, Claverdon and Henley.
547	Leamington and Marton.
548	Coventry and Coleshill via Meriden.
549	Coventry and Coleshill via Balsall and Knowle.
550	Leamington and Southam.
551	Leamington and Napton.
553	Leamington and Daventry.
554	Leamington and Bishops Itchington via Harbury.
556	Leamington, Southam and Stockton.
557	Leamington and Long Itchington.
558	Leamington, Long Itchington and Stockton.
559	Coventry and Coleshill via Fillongley.
560	Rugby and Market Harborough.
562	Rugby and Leicester.
563	Rugby and Leamington via Southam.
564	Rugby, Swinford, South Kilworth and North Kilworth.
565	Hockley Heath and Knowle.
566	Coventry and Bubbenhall.
567	Leamington and Coventry via Cubbington.
568	Leamington, Southam and Ladbroke.
569	Coventry and Balsall.
570	Rugby, Kilsby and Long Buckby.
571	Rugby and Leamington via Princethorpe.
572	Rugby and Daventry via Braunstone.
573	Rugby and Napton.
574	Rugby and Guilsborough via West Haddon.
575	Rugby and Daventry via Kilsby.
576	Rugby, Bourton and Birdingbury.
577	Rugby, Lutterworth and Walcote.
578	Rugby, Crick and West Haddon.
579	Rugby, Clifton, Lilbourne and Yelvertoft.
581	Coventry and Warwick via Kenilworth (Castle).
582	Rugby and Kings Newnham.
583	Rugby, Easenhall, Brinklow and Coventry.
584	Coventry, Rugby and Hillmorton via Ryton and Wolston.
585	Coventry and Rugby via Brinklow.
586	Coventry, Rugby and Hillmorton via Brandon and Wolston.
587	Coventry and Leamington via Stoneleigh, Bubbenhall and Cubbington.
588	Coventry and Leamington via Stoneleigh and Stare Bridge.
589	Coventry, Rugby and Hillmorton via Dunchurch.
590	Coventry and Warwick via Kenilworth (Clock).
591	Coventry and Warwick via Kenilworth (Wyandotte Inn).
592	Rugby B.T.H. and Cawston.
593	Rugby and Grandborough.
594	Rugby and Winwick via Yelvertoft.
595	Rugby, Lutterworth, Gilmorton and Walton-by-Kimcote via Churchover and Shawell.
596	Coventry, Princethorpe, Southam and Napton.
597	Tamworth, Nuneaton, Coventry and Hatton.
598	Leicester, Illston-on-the-Hill and Goadby.

Service Number	ROUTE
599	Leicester, Scraptoft and Hungarton.
600	Leicester and Croft.
601	Leicester and Enderby.
602	Leicester and Narborough.
603	Leicester and Broughton Astley.
604	Leicester and Cosby.
605	Leicester and Whetstone.
606	Horninghold, Hallaton and Market Harborough.
607	Leicester and Billesdon.
608	Leicester and Beeby.
609	Leicester and Billesdon via Illston.
610	Leicester, Bitteswell and Lutterworth.
611	Leicester, Oadby and Great Glen.
612	Leicester and Market Harborough via East Langton.
613	Leicester and Market Harborough via Great Bowden.
614	Leicester, Hallaton and Horninghold.
615	Leicester, Oadby, Great Glen and Burton Overy.
616	Leicester and Uppingham via Billesdon.
617	Leicester and Syston.
618	Leicester, Syston and Queniboro'.
619	Leicester, Syston, Rearsby and Thrussington.
620	Leicester, Broughton Astley, Dunton Bassett and Lutterworth.
621	Melton Mowbray and Braunston via Whissendine and Oakham.
622	Leicester, Twyford and Melton Mowbray.
623	Leicester, Twyford and Oakham via Somerby.
624	Melton Mowbray, Somerby and Oakham via Knossington.
625	Leicester, Mountsorrel and Loughborough via Red Hill.
626	Leicester and Loughborough via Birstall Village.
627	Leicester (Newarke) and Loughborough via Mountsorrel.
628	Leicester and Loughborough via Main Road.
629	Leicester, Sileby, Barrow and Loughborough via Rothley House.
630	Leicester and Melton Mowbray via Asfordby.
631	Leicester and Newtown Linford via Glenfield Turn.
632	Leicester and Newtown Linford via Anstey Gorse.
634	Leicester, Glenfield and Ratby.
635	Whetstone and Barwell.
636	Leicester and Desford, Bagworth and Nailstone Collieries.
637	Leicester, Huncote, Sapcote and Hinckley.
638	Leicester, Arnesby and Welford.
639	Leicester, Fleckney and Saddington.
640	Leicester and Medbourne.
641	Leicester, Kimcote and Lutterworth.
642	Leicester, Frolesworth and Claybrook Magna.
643	Leicester and Willoughby Waterless.
644	Leicester, Rearsby and Gaddesby.
645	Leicester, Thurlaston and Earl Shilton.
646	Leicester and Cosby.
647	Leicester, Bushby and Houghton.
648	Leicester, Arnesby and Shearsby.
649	Leicester, Hoby and Asfordby via Ratcliffe.
650	Leicester and Melton Mowbray via Gaddesby.
651	Leicester and Barkby via Syston.
652	Billesdon and Market Harborough.
653	Leicester and Melton Mowbray via Billesdon.
654	Leicester and Market Harborough via Kibworth and Main Road.
655	Leicester and Sileby via Syston.
656	Fleckney and Kibworth.
657	Leicester and Oakham via Tilton.
658	Leicester, Nuneaton and Coventry.
659	Leicester and Loughborough via Syston and Sileby.

Service Number	ROUTE
660	Leicester and Tilton.
661	Leicester and Melton Mowbray.
662	Leicester, Melton Mowbray and Grantham.
663	Leicester and Lutterworth via Gilmorton.
664	Leicester, Kirby Muxloe and Bagworth.
665	Leicester and Coalville.
667	Leicester and Ashby via Ravenstone.
668	Leicester, Coalville, Ashby and Burton-on-Trent.
669	Leicester, Coalville, Coleorton and Ashby.
670	Leicester, Ibstock, Snarestone, Newton Burgoland and Shackerstone.
671	Earl Shilton and Dunton Bassett.
672	Leicester and Seagrave.
674	Coalville and Loughborough via Belton and Hathern.
675	Coalville and Loughborough via Whitwick and Shepshed.
678	Coalville, S. Leicester, Ellistown and Nailstone Collieries.
679	Coalville and Lount Colliery.
683	Coalville and Worthington via Swannington.
684	Coalville, Newbold and Worthington.
687	Coalville and Hinckley via Market Bosworth and Barwell.
689	Coalville and Melbourne via Worthington.
691	Shepshed and Loughborough via Ashby Road.
692	Coalville and Loughborough via Main Road.
693	Coalville and Shepshed.
695	Ashby, Moira and Rawdon Colliery.
697	Ashby, Market Bosworth and Nuneaton.
698	Ashby, Moira and Donisthorpe.
699	Ashby, Moira and Overseal.
700	Measham and Swepstone.
701	Ashby and Blackfordby.
702	Swadlincote and Blackfordby.
703	Burton and Ashby via Bretby and Swadlincote.
704	Burton and Ashby via Stanton and Swadlincote.
705	Burton, Swadlincote and Castle Gresley.
706	Burton, Swadlincote, Castle Gresley and Linton.
707	Burton, Swadlincote and Woodville.
708	Swadlincote and Castle Gresley.
709	Swadlincote and Woodville.
710	Swadlincote and Linton.
712	Burton, Swadlincote, Donisthorpe and Measham via Midway and Albert Village.
714	Swadlincote and Donisthorpe via Albert Village.
715	Measham, Rawdon and Cut End Collieries.
716	Swadlincote and Measham via Castle Gresley and Overseal.
717	Midway and Overseal via Swadlincote and Albert Village.
718	Swadlincote and Cadley Hill.
719	Swadlincote and Overseal via Albert Village.
720	Swadlincote and Overseal via Castle Gresley.
721	Coton, Rawdon Colliery and Donisthorpe.
722	Ashby, Measham and Appleby Magna.
725	Nuneaton, Hinckley and Leicester.
726	Nuneaton and Hinckley.
727	Nuneaton and Earl Shilton.
728	Dordon and Barwell via Atherstone.
729	Hinckley and Markfield Sanatorium.
730	Nuneaton and Stoke Golding.
731	Nuneaton and Market Bosworth.
732	Ansley Buildings and Hinckley.
733	Stockingford and Newdigate Colliery.
734	Chapel End and Arley Colliery.
735	Nuneaton and Barnacle.

1904-7. Double-deck omnibus operated experimentally for 3 years and then rejected as " ahead of its time "

1912. The first omnibus type adopted by the Midland " Red " Company for regular service in Birmingham

D

1914. Tilling Stevens petrol electric single-deck omnibus

1920. Further development of the Tilling Stevens petrol electric single-deck omnibus

Service Number	ROUTE
737	Church End and Arley.
738	Nuneaton and Ansley.
739	Nuneaton and Arley.
740	Nuneaton and Gun Hill.
741	Nuneaton, Fillongley, Corley and Coventry.
743	Nuneaton and Witherley.
744	Nuneaton, Arley and Coleshill.
745	Nuneaton and Bedworth.
746	Bedworth and Smorrall Lane.
747	Nuneaton, Bedworth and Foleshill.
748	Bedworth and New Keresley.
749	Bedworth and Bulkington.
751	Hinckley and Stoney Stanton via Sharnford.
752	Hinckley and Stoke Golding.
753	Hinckley, Wolvey and Copston Magna.
754	Nuneaton and Lutterworth.
755	Hinckley, Sapcote and Stoney Stanton.
756	Sapcote and Barwell via Elmsthorpe.
760	Nuneaton and Withybrook.
762	Nuneaton, Wolvey and Copston Magna.
764	Atherstone and Polesworth via Pinwall.
765	Coventry, Nuneaton, Atherstone, Tamworth and Lichfield.
767	Nuneaton and Bulkington.
768	Atherstone and Polesworth via Dordon and Grendon.
770	Atherstone and Ratcliffe Culey.
771	Nuneaton and Atherstone via Ridge Lane.
772	Wilnecote and Nuneaton (Courtaulds).
773	Gun Hill, Arley, Corley and Coventry.
774	Fillongley and Coventry via Corley Moor.
775	Atherstone and Birmingham via Coleshill.
776	Tamworth and Wood End Pit.
778	Atherstone, Twycross and Norton.
779	Atherstone and Baxterley.
780	Tamworth and Standard Motor Works.
781	Dordon and Pooley Hall Colliery.
782	Tamworth and Polesworth.
783	Tamworth, Polesworth and Dordon.
784	Tamworth, Polesworth and Warton.
785	Warton and Hall End Colliery.
786	Tamworth and Wilnecote.
787	Tamworth and Tamworth Colliery.
788	Tamworth and Hall End Colliery.
789	Tamworth and Coventry via Kingsbury and Arley.
790	Tamworth and Kingsbury.
791	Tamworth and Hurley.
792	Tamworth and Leicester via Market Bosworth.
793	Tamworth and Elford.
794	Dordon and Hinckley via Atherstone.
795	Tamworth and Middleton.
796	Tamworth and Amington.
797	Tamworth, Shuttington and Austrey.
798	Tamworth, Kingsbury and Piccadilly.
799	Tamworth and Birchmoor.
800	Tamworth and Mile Oak.
801	Tamworth, Mile Oak, Hints and Lichfield.
802	Mile Oak and Pooley Hall Colliery.
803	Tamworth and Burton via Coton-in-the-Elms.
804	Tamworth and Clifton Campville.
807	Tamworth, Harlaston and Edingale.
810	Burton and Kings Bromley via Dunstall and Yoxall.

Routes 812-917

Service Number	ROUTE
812	Burton and Rugeley via Dunstall and Hamstall Ridware.
813	Burton and Hamstall Ridware.
814	Burton, Barton and Yoxall.
815	Burton and Barton-under-Needwood.
817	Burton and Dunstall.
818	Watford Gap, Little Hay, Wall and Lichfield.
819	Elford and Lichfield.
820	Burton, Dunstall and Forester Arms.
822	Lichfield and Whittington.
823	Stafford, Rugeley and Lichfield via Little Haywood.
824	Stafford and Rugeley via Little Haywood.
825	Stafford, Rugeley and Lichfield via Main Road.
826	Stafford and Rugeley via Main Road.
828	Burton and Abbots Bromley via Main Road and Hoar Cross.
829	Burton and Abbots Bromley via Rangemore and Hoar Cross.
831	Stafford, Little Haywood and Colwich Station.
832	Stafford and Hednesford.
833	Rugeley and Brereton.
834	Stafford and Cannock Chase (R.A.F.).
836	Stafford, Huntington and Cannock.
837	Cannock and Huntington.
838	Stafford, Penkridge and Cannock.
840	Penkridge and Huntington.
843	Rugeley, Brereton and Upper Longdon.
852	Stafford and Hopton.
870	Newport and Outwoods.
871	Stafford and Newport via Doxey, Beffcote and Bramstead.
874	Stafford, Hyde Lea and Longridge.
880	Wolverhampton, Hurst Hill and Oldbury.
881	Wolverhampton and Hurst Hill.
882	Stourbridge and Wolverhampton.
883	Wolverhampton and Kinver.
884	Wolverhampton and Kidderminster.
885	Wolverhampton, Stourbridge and Kidderminster.
886	Dawley and Hadley (Castle Works).
887	Wellington and Shirlett Sanatorium.
889	Dawley, and Donnington (Central Ordnance Depot).
890	Madeley, Ironbridge and Donnington (C.O.D.).
895	Wolverhampton and Wellington.
896	Wellington, Ironbridge and Madeley.
897	Wellington, Dawley, Madeley and Ironbridge.
898	Dawley, Lord Hill and Bicton Heath via Leighton and Shrewsbury.
899	Wellington, Oakengates and St. Georges.
900	Wellington and Oakengates.
901	Wellington, Horsehay, Broseley and Bridgnorth.
902	Shrewsbury and Bridgnorth via Ironbridge and Buildwas.
903	Wellington, Ironbridge and Broseley.
904	Wellington, Broseley and Much Wenlock.
905	Wellington and Dawley.
906	Wellington and Madeley.
907	Wellington and Lawley Bank.
908	Wellington and Church Stretton.
909	Wellington, Madeley, Ironbridge, Bridgnorth and Kidderminster.
910	Bridgnorth, Morville, Monkhopton and Netchwood.
911	Bridgnorth and Much Wenlock.
912	Wellington and Newport.
913	Wellington, Donnington and Muxton Turn.
914	Wellington and Trench.
915	Wellington and Donnington (Roundabout).
917	Newport and Edgmond.

Service Number	ROUTE
918	Wellington, Madeley and Kemberton.
919	Wellington, Sutton Moddock and Bridgnorth.
920	Wellington and Little Dawley.
923	Wellington and Great Bolas.
924	Wellington and Ellerdine via Longden and Crudgington.
925	Shrewsbury, High Ercall, Cold Hatton and Wellington.
926	Shrewsbury, Atcham and Wellington.
927	Shrewsbury, Shawbury, High Ercall and Wellington.
928	Shrewsbury and Market Drayton via Shawbury and Tern Hill.
929	Shrewsbury and Stanton Village.
931	Shrewsbury and Shawbury Aerodrome.
936	Shrewsbury, Condover and Ryton.
944	Shrewsbury and Montford Bridge.
953	Shrewsbury, Fitz and Grafton Village.
954	Shrewsbury and High Ercall.
955	Shrewsbury and Church Stretton.
958	Shrewsbury, Longdon and Pulverbatch.
959	Shrewsbury and Minsterley.
960	Shrewsbury, Minsterley and Plox Green.
962	Shrewsbury and Shirlett Sanatorium.
963	Shrewsbury and Much Wenlock via Cound Harley.
964	Shrewsbury and Bridgnorth via Cound Harley.
965	Shrewsbury and Cound Village.
966	Shrewsbury and Cross Houses.
967	Shrewsbury and Broseley via Cross Houses.
968	Shrewsbury and Madeley via Cross Houses and Cressage.
969	Shrewsbury and Broseley via Cross Houses and Cound Harley.
970	Shrewsbury and Brockton via Cross Houses, Cound Harley and Much Wenlock.
975	Shrewsbury and Broseley via Ironbridge.
976	Shrewsbury, Baschurch, Ruyton and Wykey.
977	Shrewsbury and Oswestry via Ruyton.
978	Shrewsbury and Oswestry via Nesscliff.
979	Shrewsbury and Oswestry via Nesscliff and Whittington.
981	Shrewsbury and Ellesmere via Myddle and Cockshutt.
984	Shrewsbury and Nesscliff.
990	Shrewsbury, Leebrockhurst and Weston.
991	Shrewsbury and Sutton Road (War. Ag. Committee).

LOCAL AND TOWN SERVICES

Service Number	ROUTE
A.1	Bromsgrove and Longbridge via Sidemoor.
A.2	Bromsgrove and Longbridge via Catshill.
A.3	Hagley and Longbridge.
A.4	Dodford and Longbridge.
A.5	Ford Lane (Bromsgrove) and Longbridge.
A.21	Bath Road (Worcester) and Longbridge.
A.22	St. Nicholas Street (Worcester) and Longbridge.
A.23	Newport Street (Worcester) and Longbridge.
A.24	Droitwich and Longbridge.
B.1	Banbury and Easington.
B.2	Banbury and Old Grimsbury.
B.3	Banbury and Warwick Road.
B.4	Banbury and Grimsbury.
B.10	Banbury and N.A.C.
B.81	Birmingham and Windmill Lane.
B.82	Birmingham and Bearwood via Dudley Road.
B.83	Birmingham and Soho via Heath Street.
B.84	Birmingham and St. Paul's Road.
B.85	Birmingham and Spon Lane.
B.86	Birmingham and Oldbury via Dudley Road.
B.87	Birmingham and Dudley via Dudley Road.
B.88	Dudley, Oldbury and Windmill Lane.
C.76	Coalville, Peggs Green, Griflydam and Coleorton.
C.77	Coalville and Whitwick Circular.
C.78	Coalville and Ellistown Church.
C.79	Coalville and Battram Villa.
C.80	Coalville and Bagworth.
C.82	Coalville and Blackwood Road.
C.88	Coalville and Monastery Cross Roads.
C.89	Coalville and Desford Colliery via Bagworth.
C.95	Coalville and Ravenstone via Standard Hill.
D.1	Dudley and Priory Estate (Forest Road).
D.2	Dudley and Priory Estate (Gorse Road).
D.3	Dudley and Watsons Green Estate.
D.4	Dudley and Netherton via Grazebrook Estate.
D.6	Dudley and Gornal Wood via Himley Road.
D.7	Dudley and Grace Mary Estate via Oakham and Dixons Green.
D.9	Dudley and Cradley Heath via Dudley Wood.
D.11	Dudley and Priory Estate (Mayfield Road).
D.40	Dudley and Gornal Wood.
E.1	Evesham and Hampton (School).
E.2	Evesham and Deacle Place.
E.3	Evesham and Fairfield Estate.
H.1	Hereford and White Cross.
H.2	Hereford and Westfields via Holmer Memorial.
H.3	Hereford and Breinton Road.
H.4	Hereford and Tupsley Pitch.
H.5	Hereford and College Road.
H.6	Hereford and Munstone via College Road.
H.7	Hereford and Hunderton.
H.8	Hereford and St. Martins.
H.9	Hereford and Redhill Avenue.
H.11	Hereford and Three Elms via White Cross.
H.12	Hereford and Westfields via White Cross.

Service Number	ROUTE
H.14	Hereford and Holmer Cross Roads.
H.15	Hereford and College Road.
H.10	Hereford and Rotherwas.
H.20	Barrs Court Station and Rotherwas.
H.21	Hinckley, Burbage and Three Pots Inn.
H.23	Hinckley and Wykin Village.
H.24	Hinckley and Elwell Avenue (Barwell) via Leicester Road.
H.25	Hinckley (Regent Street) and Woodland Road.
H.26	Hinckley and Burbage (via Sketchley Road).
H.27	Hinckley and Tudor Road via Derby Road.
H.28	Hinckley and Tudor Road (corner of Stanley Road).
H.29	Hinckley and Burbage via Sketchley.
H.30	Hinckley and Burbage (Freemans Lane).
H.31	Hinckley and Burbage (Lutterworth Road).
H.32	Hinckley and Burbage (Liberal Club).
H.33	Hinckley and Three Pots.
H.37	Hinckley and Earl Shilton via Barwell.
K.1	Kidderminster and Sutton Farm Estate Circular.
K.2	Kidderminster and Sutton Farm Estate Circular.
K.3	Broadwaters and H. Cheshire's School, Habberley Road.
K.5	Kidderminster and Sion Hill (Sion Avenue).
K.6	Kidderminster and Greenhill (Vine Street).
K.7	Kidderminster and Somerleyton.
K.8	Kidderminster and Aggborough.
K.9	Kidderminster and Trimpley via Habberley Valley.
K.10	Kidderminster and Lickhill via Foley Park.
K.11	Kidderminster and Bewdley.
K.12	Kidderminster and Stourport via Foley Park.
K.14	Kidderminster and Franche.
K.15	Kidderminster and Cookley.
K.16	Kidderminster and Caunsall via Cookley.
K.17	Kidderminster and Stanklyn Lane.
K.19	Stourport and Elmley Lovett.
K.20	Stourport and Lickhill.
K.21	Kidderminster and Jubilee Drive.
K.22	Kidderminster and Elmley Lovett.
L.1	Leicester (Newarke Street) and Braunstone via Narborough Road.
L.2	Leicester (Newarke Street) and Braunstone via Hinckley Road.
L.3/4	Leicester (Newarke Street) and New Found Pool.
L.5	Leicester (Newarke) and Wigston Magna via Welford Road and Saffron Lane.
L.6	Leicester (Newarke), Wigston Magna, South Wigston and Leicester (Newarke).
L.7	Leicester (Newarke), South Wigston, Wigston Magna and Leicester (Newarke).
L.8	Leicester (Newarke), South Wigston, Wigston Magna and Leicester (Northampton Square).
L.9	Leicester (Newarke) and Exeter Road.
L.10	Leicester (Northampton Square) and Wigston Magna via Oadby.
L.11	Leicester (Northampton Square) and Oadby only.
L.12	Leicester (Newarke Street) and Ravenhurst Road.
L.13	Leicester (L.M.S. & L.N.E.R. Stns.) and Oadby Racecourse.
L.14	Leicester (Belgrave Gate) and Gilroes Cemetery.
L.15	Wigston and Enderby.
L.17	Oadby and Markfield Sanatorium.
L.18	Leicester (Northampton Square) and Wigston Magna via Welford Road.
L.19	Leicester (Western B'vard) and Kirby Muxloe.
L.20	Leicester (Belgrave Gate) and Humberstone Lane via Melton Road.

Service Number	ROUTE
L.21	Leicester (Belgrave Gate) and Humberstone Lane via Marfitt Street.
L.22	Leicester (Newarke Street) and Kingsway.
L.23	Leicester (Newarke Street) and Countesthorpe via Blaby.
L.24	Leicester (Newarke) and Countesthorpe via South Wigston.
L.26	Leicester (Belgrave Gate) and Highway Road.
L.27	Leicester (Newarke) and Blaby.
L.29	Leicester (Belgrave Gate) and Scraptoft.
L.34	Leicester (Belgrave Gate) and Anstey via Glenfield Turn.
L.35	Leicester (Belgrave Gate) and Anstey via Gorse.
L.40	Leamington and Old Milverton.
L.41	Warwick, Emscote, Leamington and Rushmore Estate.
L.42	Warwick, Emscote, Leamington and Lockheed Works.
L.43	Warwick, Emscote, Leamington and Radford Road.
L.44	Warwick, Emscote and Leamington.
L.45	Leamington, Myton and Warwick (The Packmores).
L.46	Leamington and Heathcote Terrace via Whitnash.
L.47	Leamington and Windmill Corner.
L.48	Leamington and Cubbington.
L.49	Leamington and Bishops Tackbrook.
L.50	Barford and Warwick (Packmores).
M.10	Malvern Link and British Camp via Malvern Wells.
M.11	Malvern Link and British Camp via Wyche.
M.12	Great Malvern and Belmont.
M.14	Great Malvern and Wedderburn Road via Belmont.
M.15	Great Malvern and Poolbrook.
M.16	Great Malvern and West Malvern.
M.17	Great Malvern and Wyche Cutting.
M.18	Great Malvern and St. Andrew's Road.
M.19	Great Malvern and Barnards Green via Station.
M.21	Great Malvern and British Camp.
M.22	Great Malvern and Malvern Link via Belmont.
M.23	Great Malvern Circular.
M.24	Great Malvern and Barnards Green via Belmont and Link.
M.25	Great Malvern and Poolbrook via Sherrards Green.
M.26	Great Malvern and Wedderburn Road via Sherrards Green.
M.27	Great Malvern and Colwall via Wyche Cutting.
M.28	Great Malvern and Upper Welland via Malvern Wells.
M.29	Great Malvern and St. Andrew's Road via Sherrards Green.
M.30	Great Malvern and Wedderburn Road via Station.
M.33	Great Malvern and Merebrook.
M.34	Great Malvern and Guarlford Church.
N.32	Nuneaton and Chapel End via Round Towers.
N.33	Nuneaton and Chapel End via Haunchwood Road.
N.34	Nuneaton and Stockingford Station via Round Towers.
N.35	Nuneaton and Stockingford Station via Haunchwood Road.
N.36	Nuneaton and Round Towers.
N.37	Nuneaton and Stockingford Station via Heath End Road.
N.42	Nuneaton and Galley Common via Tuttle Hill and Chapel End.
N.44	Nuneaton and Weddington.
N.45	Nuneaton and Hartshill via Tuttle Hill.
N.47	Nuneaton and Ansley Buildings.
N.48	Nuneaton and Chapel End via Tuttle Hill.
N.52	Nuneaton (Middlemarch Road) and Higham Lane.
R.2	Redditch and Saiters Lane.
R.3	Redditch and Bransons Cross.
R.4	Redditch and Feckenham via Mutton Hall.
R.5	Redditch and Studley via Crabbs Cross.

Service Number	ROUTE
R.6	Redditch and Crabbs Cross.
R.7	Redditch and New End via Astwood Bank.
R.8	Redditch and Studley via Green Lane.
R.9	Redditch and Hill Top.
R.10	Redditch and Weatheroak via Rowney Green.
R.12	Redditch and Feckenham Road.
R.14	Redditch and Feckenham via New End.
R.15	Redditch and Alcester via Crabbs Cross.
R.16	Redditch and Sambourne.
R.17	Redditch and Red Lane.
R.18	Redditch and Hunt End.
R.19	Redditch and Upper Bentley via Hill Top.
R.22	Redditch and Web Heath.
R.27	Redditch and Alvechurch.
R.28	Redditch and Alcester via Studley and Greenlands.
R.38	Redditch and Greenlands Estate via Sillins Avenue.
R.72	Rugby and Corbett Street via Warwick Street.
R.73	Rugby and New Bilton.
R.74	Rugby and Southfields Estate.
R.75	Rugby and Ashlawn Estate.
R.76	Rugby and Long Lawford.
R.77	Old Bilton, Rugby and Hillmorton.
R.78	Rugby and Hillmorton.
R.79	Rugby and Clifton Inn.
R.81	Hillmorton, Rugby and Old Bilton.
R.82	Rugby and Newton.
R.84	Rugby and Barby Camp via Dunchurch.
R.85	Rugby and St. Cross Hospital.
R.86	Rugby and Church Lawford.
R.87	Rugby and Lower Hillmorton.
R.89	Clifton, Rugby and Croop Hill.
R.91	Rugby and Thurlaston via Old Bilton and Dunchurch.
R.92	Rugby and Brownsover.
R.93	Rugby and Thurlaston via Dunchurch and Main Road.
S.1	Shrewsbury and Abbots Road.
S.3	Shrewsbury and Copthorne via Barracks.
S.4	Shrewsbury and Column.
S.5	Shrewsbury and Weeping Cross.
S.6	Shrewsbury and Greenfields Street.
S.7	Shrewsbury and Cross Hills.
S.8	Shrewsbury and Cemetery (Kennedy Road).
S.9	Shrewsbury and Ditherington.
S.10	Shrewsbury and Harlescott Village.
S.11	Shrewsbury and Battlefield.
S.12	Shrewsbury and Castlefields.
S.13	Shrewsbury and Copthorne via Woodfield Road.
S.14	Shrewsbury and Sundorne Avenue.
S.15	Shrewsbury and Ditherington (New Works).
S.16	Shrewsbury and Bayston Hill.
S.17	Shrewsbury and Grove Lane.
S.18	Shrewsbury and Cemetery.
S.19	Shrewsbury and Lythwood Hall.
S.20	Shrewsbury and Meole Village.
S.21	Shrewsbury and Underdale Avenue.
S.22	Shrewsbury and Abbotsfield.
S.23	Shrewsbury and Roman Road.
S.24	Shrewsbury and Meole Brooklands.
S.25	Shrewsbury and Bicton Heath.

Service Number	ROUTE
S.33	Stourbridge and Lye Cross.
S.34	Stourbridge and The Hayes.
S.36	Stourbridge and Colley Gate.
S.37	Stourbridge and Wynall Estate via Station, Ludgbridge Brook and Careless Green.
S.38	Stourbridge and Wynall Estate via Lye Cross and Careless Green.
S.41	Stourbridge and New Wood via Wollaston.
S.50	Stourbridge and Wollaston via The Heath.
S.51	Stourbridge and Wollaston (Ridge Street).
S.53	Stourbridge and Norton.
S.56	Stourbridge and The Heath (Harmon Road).
S.62	Chester Road and Boldmere.
S.63	Chester Road and Sutton via Boldmere.
S.65	Chester Road and Sutton via Walmley.
S.67	Erdington and Beggars Bush via Goosemoor Lane.
S.69	Chester Road and Sutton via Wylde Green.
S.70	Chester Road, Sutton and Ashfurlong Corner via Whitehouse Common
S.71	Erdington and Ashfurlong Corner via Walmley.
S.72	Sutton and Minworth.
S.73	Chester Road and Parson & Clerk.
S.76	Erdington and Parson & Clerk via Court Lane.
S.77	Stafford and Milford.
S.78	Stafford, Weeping Cross and Stockton Lane.
S.79	Stafford, Milford and Brocton Village.
S.80	Stafford, Weeping Cross and Walton Village.
S.81	Stafford and Weeping Cross.
S.82	Doxey, L.M.S. Station, Stafford and Common Station.
S.83	Stafford and Common Station.
S.84	Stafford and Doxey.
S.85	Stafford and Lotus Works via Sandon Road.
S.86	Stafford, Lotus Works and Fonthil Road via Sandon Road.
S.87	Stafford and Lotus Works via Corporation Street.
S.88	Stafford and Castlechurch.
S.89	Stafford, Littleworth and Kingston Hill.
S.90	Stafford and Littleworth (Circular).
S.91	Stafford and Littleworth (Direct).
S.92	Stafford, Littleworth and Kingston Hill via Lichfield Road.
S.93	Stafford and Coton Fields.
S.94	Stafford, Rising Brook and Silkmore Hall.
S.95	Stafford, Rising Brook and Silkmore Lane.
S.96	Stafford, Rising Brook and Moss Pit.
S.97	Stafford, Rising Brook, Moss Pit and Acton Trussell.
S.98	Stafford, Rising Brook and Hyde Lea.
S.99	Stafford, Rising Brook, Silkmore Lane and Rickerscote.
W.1	Worcester Cross and Ombersley Road.
W.2	Worcester Cross and Checketts Lane. (Droitwich Road.)
W.3	Angel Place and Bromyard Road.
W.4	Angel Place and Malvern Road.
W.5	Worcester Cross and Rainbow Hill.
W.6	Worcester Cross and London Road.
W.9	Worcester Cross and Tolladine Road.
W.10	Worcester Cross and Bath Road.
W.11	Angel Place and Bransford Road.
W.12	Angel Place and Comer Gardens.
W.14	Worcester Cross and Blackpole Road.
W.15	Worcester Cross and Astwood Road.
W.16	Angel Place and Bromwich Road.
W.17	Worcester Cross and Wylds Lane.
W.19	Angel Place and Martley Turn.

[*Photo : J. Whitlock*

1922. Tilling Stevens petrol electric front-entrance omnibus with " knife-board " seating arrangement on the upper deck

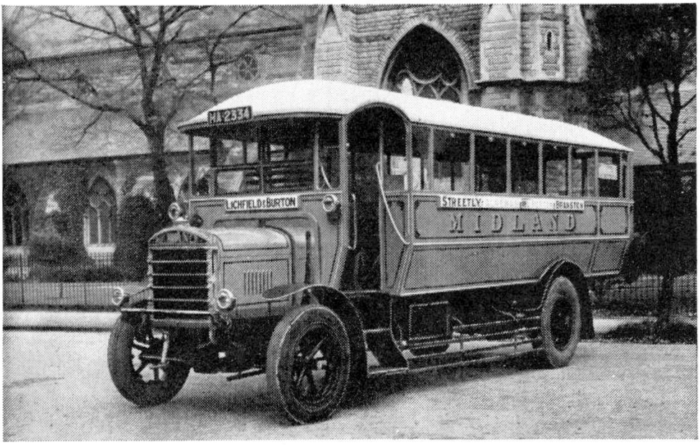

1924-5. The first " SOS " type 31-seater omnibus, fitted with pneumatic tyres

[Photo : Brush Elect. Eng. Co. Ltd.

1926. A further development of the "SOS" type. This vehicle incorporates forward steering arrangement and seats 34 persons

1927. "Q" type single-deck omnibus, seating 37 passengers

Routes W22-W41

Service Number	ROUTE
W.22	Worcester Cross and Droitwich Road. (Claines Lane.)
W.23	Angel Place and Bromyard Road.
W.24	Worcester Cross and Blackpole (Hindlip Road).
W.25	Worcester Cross and Brickfields via Rainbow Hill.
W.29	Worcester (Newport Street) and Hallow via Hylton Road.
W.40	Wellington and Wicketts Inn.
W.41	Arleston Estate and Orleton Lane (Schools).

THE EVOLUTION OF THE MIDLAND "RED" OMNIBUS

MENTION was made on an earlier page of the fact that The Midland "Red" adopted the motor omnibus as its standard form of transport in 1912. The type of vehicle which the Midland "Red" Company adopted for general use in that year was the Tilling Stevens "petrol-electric" (page 16). Its name originated from the fact that it was not equipped with the now common arrangement of engine and gearbox. The engine, although it was of the normal petrol propulsion type, was coupled to a large dynamo, and the electricity thereby generated provided power for a large electric motor which propelled the vehicle. This type of vehicle continued in general use up to 1924, being mounted in buses both of single deck and double deck type, all operating on solid tyres.

The evolution of the modern Midland "Red" omnibus dates from 1924. In that year the Company decided to build its own vehicles, and the vehicle known as the "SOS" was developed (page 25). The 4-cylinder "SOS" petrol engine was designed and produced, and the new vehicle's chassis was equipped with Giant pneumatic tyres which were then being introduced for heavy vehicles. The electric drive was discarded, to be replaced by the ordinary gearbox drive. With this type of vehicle the normal steering arrangement was employed, with the driver's compartment placed behind the engine, and there were 31 passenger seats. A modification of this design appeared in 1926, when the Company decided to develop an "SOS" vehicle with a forward steering arrangement. In this version the driver's compartment was moved forward to the offside of the engine, thereby releasing more room in the body of the vehicle for passenger seats, which were increased to 34 in number (page 26).

The "Q" type vehicle (page 26) was the next of the Company's designs to take the road, its service dating from 1927. The noteworthy feature of the new type was the rearrangement of the seating, which made it possible to provide accommodation for 37 passengers as opposed to the previous maximum capacity of 34.

Hitherto Giant single pneumatic tyres had been used for both front and rear axles, but in 1928 they were replaced by smaller tubes. This development was the principle feature of the 37-seater "QL" type of omnibus (page 43) which distinguished it from its predecessors. This vehicle, which was designed and built in 1928, was also the first of the Company's omnibuses to employ twin tyres instead of single tubes on the rear axle. The reduced overall diameter of the wheels had the effect of lowering the height of the chassis frame, thereby modernising its general appearance. The seating was again rearranged, and a new type of seat introduced to afford greater passenger comfort ; there was, however, a consequent reduction of the seating capacity to 35. This vehicle was the last type to be produced with straight side panels.

The following year saw the introduction of the vehicle known as the "M" type (page 44), with 34 seats, which was the first design to have curved side panels swept below the level of the chassis frame. This development enhanced materially the vehicle's appearance, and provided a lower loading line.

No mention has yet been made of a type of motor transport which was being developed concurrently with that of the omnibus. From the inception of the motor omnibus for ordinary stage carriage passenger transport operation, the Company had borne in mind the desirability of producing special vehicles for touring and the carriage of the purely pleasure-seeking type of passenger, and a number of vehicles of this type were built. The vehicle known as the "charabanc" was in general use for this purpose up to 1927, at first as a Tilling Stevens petrol electric vehicle, operating on solid tyres, with a special type of body housing rows of upholstered seats, access to each row being gained by a separate hinged door on the nearside.

In 1925 this type of body, varying little from its predecessors, was mounted on an ordinary "SOS" chassis, and functioned very suitably for its purpose. The principal disadvantage of this type of vehicle was that, apart from a folding hood which could be erected only with difficulty in inclement weather, the passengers were exposed entirely to the elements, as no side screening arrangement was fitted. In 1926 the forward steering type of charabanc body was employed, this being similar to that of its immediate predecessor with the exception that a forward steering arrangement was used, as on the 1926 type service bus.

A much improved type of touring coach was devised by the Company in 1927. This, the "QC" type, was vastly different from the charabanc. A new and better type of folding hood was employed, and fixed glass screens or windows were fitted on both sides of the vehicle ; there was, furthermore, a single entrance at the front of the vehicle, on the nearside, from which a central gangway provided passage to the seats. The driver sat with the passengers in the body of the vehicle, the normal steering arrangement being utilised. This special type of coach body was mounted on the " Q " type " SOS " chassis.

The " QC " coach became, in the following year, the " QLC " coach (page 87)—that is to say, an exactly similar type of coach body was mounted on the " QL " type chassis, with its smaller pneumatic tyres and twin tyres on the rear axle. It was in this period that the Company introduced extended 5-day and 12-day tours, and these " QC " and " QLC " coaches were found to be eminently suitable for this particular purpose. Long distance services to towns well outside the Company's area of operation, and to the seaside, were also inaugurated, and the need for a special vehicle for this purpose, providing greater passenger comfort, became apparent.

To meet this demand a special long-distance coach known as the " XL " was built in 1929, the new design being modified somewhat in the following year, and the type designation being changed to " RR " (page 44). The " RR " type incorporated several new refinements, including more comfortable seats, more elaborate interior decorations, and a fixed roof similar to the standard single deck passenger omnibus. A notable feature of its equipment was the 6-cylinder petrol engine, designed and produced by the Company.

The power plant of the " RR " type made it the precursor of a further stage in the development of Midland " Red " vehicles, for in 1930 the Company decided to build a number of single deck omnibuses employing a 6-cylinder engine instead of the 4-cylinder " SOS " engine, use of which had been standardised in omnibuses, charabancs and coaches since 1924. These 6-cylinder single deck omnibuses were primarily intended for use on what are known as " express" services, where the number of stops is limited, but the passenger seating arrangement remained practically the same as in the " M " type. The type of 6-cylinder engine used in the " MM " (page 45), as this new vehicle was designated, was also fitted to the " QLC " coach referred to above.

Between 1930 and 1933, the " IM4 " type single deck omnibus (page 45) was produced in large numbers. This was an ordinary 34-seater single deck omnibus with a 4-cylinder engine, intended for ordinary stage carriage work, with an improved type of body providing greater passenger comfort, particularly from the point of view of the upholstery of the seats. Hide had been used almost exclusively hitherto, but moquette was now introduced; and from that date it became the standard type of upholstery for all vehicles produced by the Company. Concurrently with the production of the " IM4," the " IM6 " vehicle was introduced — a very similar type to the " IM4 " except that a 6-cylinder petrol engine was employed.

The year 1933 also saw the introduction of a few 6-cylinder engined single-deck omnibuses fitted with a similar, though somewhat smaller, type of 6-cylinder engine as used in the " RR " long distance coaches. These vehicles were known as the " BRR " type.

In 1934 and 1935, the " RR " type long distance coach was redesigned and developed into the " LRR " type, of which a batch was introduced into the fleet in 1935. The " LRR " type was a much improved version, mounting a body of more modern and tasteful appearance than anything yet seen, with a central entrance, an improvement largely achieved by streamlining and lower panelling. The 6-cylinder petrol engines were fitted and 30 seats were provided.

During the period of the production of the " IM4 " and " IM6 " single deck type omnibuses—that is, between 1930 and 1933—the Company decided to produce its own type of double deck omnibus for use on the more thickly populated routes within its area of operation, thus reverting to this large capacity design for the first time since 1922, when the Tilling Stevens petrol electric front entrance omnibus was produced (see p. 29).*

A 55-seater rear entrance double deck vehicle, fitted with a 6-cylinder petrol engine, and appearing in 1932 (page 46), was the first fruit of this decision. In the following year, the front entrance double deck type of vehicle was evolved (page 63), and batches of omnibuses of this type were built in the years 1934-6.

Development in 1935 was devoted once more to the sphere of the power plant. In that year the propulsion unit was changed to the 6-cylinder compression ignition type of engine, using heavy oil and further batches of the double deck bus so equipped were added to the fleet in 1938 and 1939, all of which possessed a seating capacity of 56.

But we are outrunning the development of the single deck omnibus. The newcomer to this division of the Company's fleet in 1935 was the " ON " type. Previous single deck vehicles had all been built to an overall length of 26 ft., but the " ON " type was of increased dimensions, the body being lengthened to 27 ft. 6 in. to permit the provision of 38 seats. The original " ON " was fitted with the 6-cylinder petrol engine ; a number of them were later converted to the 6-cylinder compression ignition type, and were designated " CON " (converted ON's). In 1935, a batch of " ON " vehicles was produced, fitted directly with the 6-cylinder compression ignition engine, which gained for them the classification " DON " (Diesel ON).

These various " ON " types evolved in 1936 into the " SON "

* This vehicle operated for five to six years before withdrawal.

type (page 64), which became the standard type of single deck omnibus, batches being produced in each of the years up to the outbreak of the War, the last coming off the line early in 1940.

The outbreak of the War meant a cessation in the Company's production of its own vehicles, but during the war period small numbers of standard makes of rear entrance double deck vehicles were added to the fleet, these being of Leyland, A.E.C., Guy and Daimler manufacture. Many of these vehicles will be remembered as having been equipped with the slatted, wooden type of passenger seat. These seats have been, or are being, converted into the standard moquette upholstered type of seat now in general use.

To complete the history of the Company's standard vehicles, it remains only to describe the later development stages of the Midland "Red" saloon coaches for touring. In 1935 the Company produced a further batch of open type coaches with a folding hood, known as the "OLR" type, these being an improved version of the earlier "QC" and "QLC" types. During the War period it was decided to convert these vehicles into single deck service type omnibuses, in which form they are still operating. This was done principally because the Company was badly in need of additional single deck omnibuses at that time, and because it was felt that the open type of touring coach was fast becoming obsolete.

There are two further types of touring coach to be mentioned, both produced before the War. The first of these was added to the fleet in 1937, and is known as "SLR." These vehicles were a much improved version of the "LRR," having 30 seats, and embodied a special full-fronted streamlined design. Originally fitted with 6-cylinder petrol engines, the "SLR" coaches are now being converted to 6-cylinder compression ignition engines.

The remaining type of touring coach to be mentioned is the "ONC," produced immediately before the War, this again being a much improved version of the "SLR." It is equipped with a 6-cylinder compression ignition engine, provided with 30 very comfortable seats, and has a very pleasing scheme of interior decoration.

Mention must be made of a small batch of experimental vehicles produced towards the end of the pre-war period. The main interest of these 'buses lay in the situation of the engine, which was placed behind the rear axle, and they were known as the Rear Engined type. This method of design was tried on both single deck service 'buses and on a long distance saloon touring coach similar to the "ONC" type. The "rear-engine" arrangement did not prove entirely satisfactory in operation, and during the War period the Company decided to experiment with the under-floor type of engine, located "amidships." The "rear-engine" vehicles were all converted to this under-floor engine design, being known respectively as "S.1," "S.2," "S.3," and "S.4."* The engine in these vehicles was of the 6-cylinder compression ignition type, and this particular arrangement enabled a single deck body with 40 passenger seats to be provided. This practice proved eminently successful, and these experimental 'buses with under-floor engines gave such good service during the war period that the Company decided to adopt this engine arrangement as standard for all its future single deck service omnibuses and touring coaches. So far as double deck 'buses were concerned, the Company decided, after very careful consideration of the matter, to revert to the rear entrance arrangement for all future vehicles of this type, and a rear entrance double decker prototype was produced in 1944.

The fleet numbers given in this book include the first batch of 100 single deck under-floor engined omnibuses for post-war delivery, this type being known as the "S.6." A further 200 single deck omnibuses of this type are to follow (type "S.8"). This booklet also includes the fleet numbers of the first 100 double deck omnibuses for post-war delivery. This batch of vehicles will be mounted on A.E.C. chassis. A further 100 double deck omnibuses are on order (type "REDD" A.D.2), and these will be mounted on chassis to the Company's own designs, the engine being situated in the conventional position at the front. In addition, there are on order 45 touring coaches for long distance work (type "C.1"), and 12 special coaches for the operation of extended tours (type "C.2").

The whole of the chassis for these vehicles (with the exception of the 100 A.E.C. double deck type chassis mentioned above) will be produced at the Company's Works at Carlyle Road, Edgbaston, Birmingham, to the Company's own designs, and all the single deck 'buses and coaches will be fitted with the under-floor type of engine.

The principal features of these new vehicles are the absence of engine noise, general smoothness of running, and improved road springing. Power-assisted braking is also installed, and improved destination gear and route number equipment is fitted. All vehicles will be equipped with heating systems. The Company's own design of compression ignition engine will be fitted, and in course of time, the petrol engine will be entirely superseded as a propulsion unit.

With the exception of a comparatively small number of omnibus and coach bodies which have been built from time to time at the Company's Works at Carlyle Road, Edgbaston, Birmingham, the bodies fitted to the Company's vehicles have been built by a number of body building firms, whose works are situated in different parts of the country, and this practice will be adopted so far as the new vehicles on order are concerned. All omnibus and coach bodies have been in the past, and will continue to be in the future, constructed entirely to the Company's own designs.

* A special experimental under-floor engine type known as the "S.5," embodying a "chassisless" construction, was produced towards the end of the war period.

GARAGES

The Company operates twenty-eight garages, which are listed below. The " Leopard Spot," or identification disc, appropriate to each garage is indicated on pages 32-33, together with its colourings ; these discs are affixed to the rear of the bus just above the registration number. In the list below each garage has been numbered so that the reader may pencil in the relevant garage number against each bus in the lists on pages 35-76. This numbering is not officially recognised and is merely used for abbreviation in this book.

1.	BIRMINGHAM (Bearwood)	*Garage and Workshops :* Bearwood Rd., Smethwick.
2.	BIRMINGHAM (Digbeth)	*Garage and Coach Station :* Digbeth, Birmingham.
3.	BANBURY	Canal Street.
4.	BROMSGROVE	The Strand.
5.	COALVILLE	Ashby Road.
6.	CRADLEY HEATH	Forge Lane
7.	DUDLEY	Birmingham Road.
8.	EVESHAM	Abbey Road.
9.	HARTSHILL	Brierley Hill.
10.	HEREFORD	Friar Street.
11.	HINCKLEY	Coventry Road.
12.	KIDDERMINSTER	New Road.
13.	LEAMINGTON	Old Warwick Road.
14.	LEICESTER	Southgate Street.
15.	LEICESTER	Sandacre Street.
16.	NUNEATON	Coton Road.
17.	OLDBURY	Wolverhampton Road.
18.	REDDITCH	Church Road.
19.	RUGBY	Railway Terrace.
20.	SHREWSBURY	Ditherington.
21.	STAFFORD	Newport Road.
22.	STOURBRIDGE	Foster Street.
23.	SUTTON COLDFIELD	Upper Holland Road.
24.	SWADLINCOTE	Midland Road.
25.	TAMWORTH	Aldergate.
26.	WELLINGTON	Charlton Street.
27.	WOLVERHAMPTON	Bilston Street.
28.	WORCESTER	Padmore Street.

TRAFFIC ENQUIRY OFFICES—

There are Traffic Enquiry Offices in all the above towns, and in addition at Coventry, Droitwich, Malvern, Stratford-upon-Avon, and Lichfield.

GAR

LEOPARD

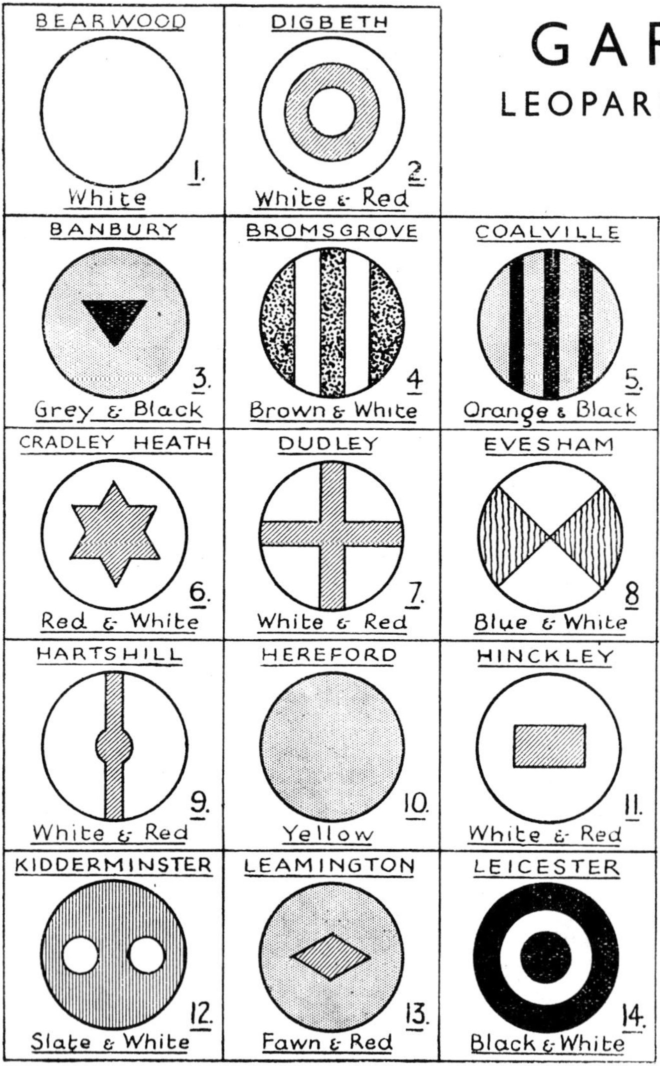
BEARWOOD
1.
White
DIGBETH
2.
White & Red
BANBURY
3.
Grey & Black
BROMSGROVE
4
Brown & White
COALVILLE
5.
Orange & Black
CRADLEY HEATH
6.
Red & White
DUDLEY
7.
White & Red
EVESHAM
8
Blue & White
HARTSHILL
9.
White & Red
HEREFORD
10.
Yellow
HINCKLEY
11.
White & Red
KIDDERMINSTER
12.
Slate & White
LEAMINGTON
13.
Fawn & Red
LEICESTER
14.
Black & White

AGE

SPOTS

SANDACRE

15. White & Black

NUNEATON

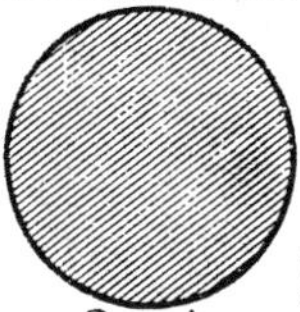

16. Red

OLDBURY

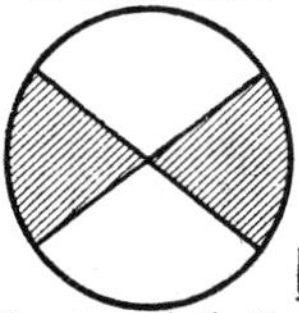

17. Red & White

REDDITCH

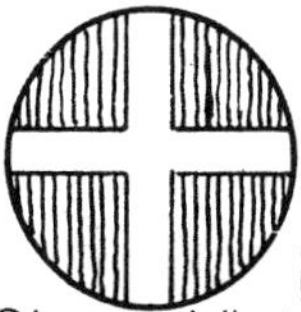

18. Blue & White

RUGBY

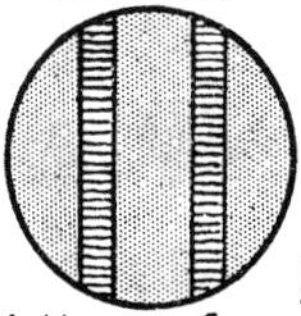

19. Yellow & Green

SHREWSBURY

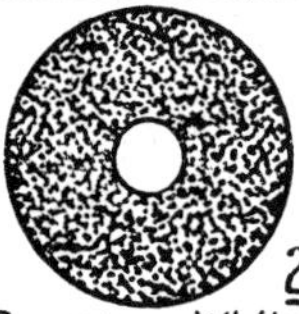

20. Brown & White

STAFFORD

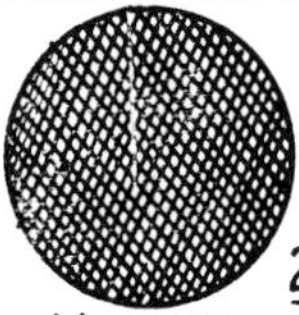

21. Mauve

STOURBRIDGE

22. Red & White

SUTTON

23. White & Red

SWADLINCOTE

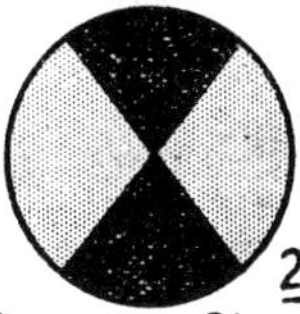

24. Orange & Black

TAMWORTH

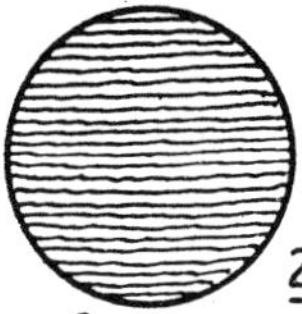

25. Green

WELLINGTON

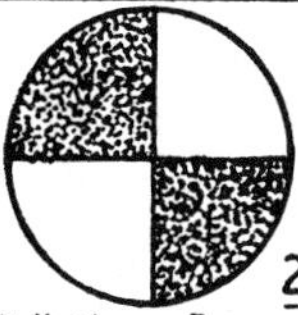

26. White & Brown

WOLVER'N

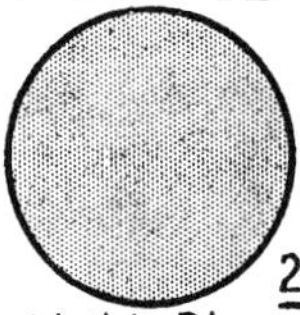

27. Light Blue

WORCESTER

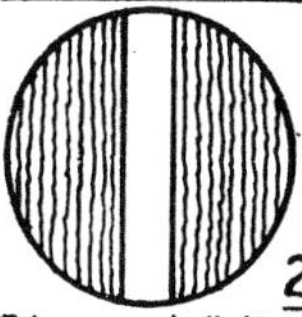

28. Blue & White

VEHICLE IDENTIFICATION NUMBERS, REGISTRATION NUMBERS, TYPES AND SEATING CAPACITIES

Fleet Number	Registration Number	Type and Seating	Garage Number
857	HA.3779	"QL" 35	
862	HA.3781	,, 35	
885	HA.4808	,, 35	
902	HA.4841	,, 35	
906	HA.4838	,, 35	
918	HA.4893	,, 35	
923	HA.4848	,, 35	
927	HA.4892	,, 35	
933	HA.4897	,, 35	
936	HA.4852	,, 35	
948	HA.4859	,, 35	
949	HA.4857	,, 35	
952	HA.4955	"M" 34	
964	HA.4874	"QL" 35	
965	HA.4875	,, 35	
970	HA.4911	"M" 34	
971	HA.4912	,, 34	
972	HA.4909	,, 34	
973	HA.4913	,, 34	
975	HA.4915	,, 34	
976	HA.4916	,, 34	
977	HA.4917	,, 34	
978	HA.4918	,, 34	
979	HA.4919	,, 34	
980	HA.4920	,, 34	
981	HA.4921	,, 34	
982	HA.4923	,, 34	
983	HA.4924	,, 34	
984	HA.4925	,, 34	
985	HA.4926	,, 34	
986	HA.4927	,, 34	
987	HA.4928	,, 34	
988	HA.4922	,, 34	
989	HA.4929	,, 34	
1001	HA.4938	,, 34	
1022	HA.4931	,, 34	

1023	HA.4932	"M"	34
1024	HA.4937	,,	34
1025	HA.4933	,,	34
1026	HA.4934	,,	34
1027	HA.4935	,,	34
1028	HA.4936	,,	34
1029	HA.4939	,,	34
1030	HA.4940	,,	34
1031	HA.4941	,,	34
1033	HA.4943	,,	34
1034	HA.4944	,,	34
1035	HA.4945	,,	34
1036	HA.4946	,,	34
1037	HA.4947	,,	34
1038	HA.4948	,,	34
1039	HA.4949	,,	34
1040	HA.4950	,,	34
1041	HA.4951	,,	34
1042	HA.4952	,,	34
1043	HA.4953	,,	34
1044	HA.4954	,,	34
1045	HA.5076	"MM"	34
1046	HA.5080	,,	34
1047	HA.5072	,,	34
1048	HA.5058	,,	34
1049	HA.5055	,,	34
1050	HA.5081	,,	34
1051	HA.5056	,,	34
1052	HA.5070	,,	34
1053	HA.5129	,,	34
1054	HA.5014	,,	34
1055	HA.5128	,,	34
1056	HA.5059	,,	34
1057	HA.5130	,,	34
1058	HA.5044	,,	34
1059	HA.5131	,,	34
1060	HA.5045	,,	34
1061	HA.5046	,,	34
1062	HA.5061	,,	34
1063	HA.5047	,,	34
1064	HA.5053	,,	34
1065	HA.5015	,,	34
1066	HA.5066	,,	34
1067	HA.5043	,,	34
1068	HA.5071	,,	34

Fleet Number	Registration Number	Type and Seating	Garage Number
1069	HA.5054	"MM" 34	
1070	HA.5064	,, 34	
1071	HA.5083	,, 34	
1072	HA.5060	,, 34	
1073	HA.5069	,, 34	
1074	HA.5132	,, 34	
1075	HA.5009	,, 34	
1076	HA.5063	,, 34	
1077	HA.5062	,, 34	
1078	HA.5057	,, 34	
1079	HA.5067	,, 34	
1080	HA.5065	,, 34	
1081	HA.5010	,, 34	
1082	HA.5134	,, 34	
1083	HA.5011	,, 34	
1084	HA.5013	,, 34	
1086	HA.5068	,, 34	
1087	HA.5052	,, 34	
1088	HA.5007	,, 34	
1089	HA.5133	,, 34	
1090	HA.5048	,, 34	
1091	HA.5049	,, 34	
1092	HA.5050	,, 34	
1093	HA.5084	,, 34	
1094	HA.5126	,, 34	
1095	HA.5051	,, 34	
1097	HA.5115	"IM4" 34	
1098	HA.5120	,, 34	
1099	HA.5112	,, 34	
1100	HA.5121	,, 34	
1101	HA.5089	,, 34	
1102	HA.5116	,, 34	
1103	HA.5118	,, 34	
1104	HA.5113	,, 34	
1107	HA.5119	,, 34	
1108	HA.5117	,, 34	
1109	HA.5086	,, 34	
1110	HA.5088	,, 34	
1111	HA.5087	,, 34	
1112	HA.5090	,, 34	
1113	HA.5091	,, 34	
1114	HA.5092	,, 34	

1115	HA.5093	" IM4 "	34
1116	HA.5085	,,	34
1117	HA.5094	,,	34
1118	HA.5097	,,	34
1119	HA.5099	,,	34
1120	HA.5100	,,	34
1121	HA.5098	,,	34
1122	HA.5101	,,	34
1123	HA.5095	,,	34
1124	HA.5096	,,	34
1125	HA.5106	,,	34
1127	HA.5110	,,	34
1129	HA.5108	,,	34
1130	HA.5109	,,	34
1131	HA.5103	,,	34
1132	HA.5104	,,	34
1134	HA.5111	,,	34
1136	HA.5012	" MM "	34
1137	HA.5127	,,	34
1138	HA.5125	,,	34
1139	HA.5073	,,	34
1140	HA.5074	,,	34
1141	HA.5075	,,	34
1142	HA.5077	,,	34
1143	HA.5078	,,	34
1144	HA.5079	,,	34
1145	HA.5082	,,	34
1148	HA.6153	" IM4 "	34
1149	HA.6154	,,	34
1150	HA.6155	,,	34
1152	HA.6157	,,	34
1153	HA.6158	,,	34
1157	HA.6162	,,	34
1158	HA.6163	,,	34
1159	HA.6164	,,	34
1161	HA.6168	,,	34
1162	HA.6166	,,	34
1163	HA.6167	,,	34
1165	HA.6170	,,	34
1166	HA.6169	,,	34
1167	HA.6171	,,	34
1168	HA.6172	,,	34
1246	HA.5123	" BRR "	34
1247	HA.6176	" IM4 "	34
1248	HA.6177	,,	34

Fleet Number	Registration Number	Type and Seating		Garage Number
1249	HA.6178	" IM4 "	34	
1250	HA.6179	,,	34	
1251	HA.6180	,,	34	
1257	HA.6186	,,	34	
1258	HA.6187	,,	34	
1259	HA.6188	,,	34	
1262	HA.6191	,,	34	
1264	HA.6193	,,	34	
1265	HA.6194	,,	34	
1267	HA.6202	,,	34	
1268	HA.6196	,,	34	
1270	HA.6206	,,	34	
1272	HA.6198	,,	34	
1274	HA.6199	,,	34	
1276	HA.6205	,,	34	
1277	HA.6207	,,	34	
1278	HA.6208	,,	34	
1279	HA.6201	,,	34	
1280	HA.6209	,,	34	
1281	HA.6210	,,	34	
1282	HA.6211	,,	34	
1284	HA.6213	,,	34	
1285	HA.6215	,,	34	
1286	HA.6216	,,	34	
1287	HA.6217	,,	34	
1288	HA.6214	,,	34	
1289	HA.6218	,,	34	
1290	HA.6219	,,	34	
1291	HA.6220	,,	34	
1292	HA.6221	,,	34	
1293	HA.6222	,,	34	
1294	HA.6223	,,	34	
1295	HA.6224	,,	34	
1296	HA.6225	,,	34	
1297	HA.6227	" IM6 "	34	
1298	HA.6228	,,	34	
1299	HA.6229	,,	34	
1300	HA.6233	,,	34	
1301	HA.6230	,,	34	
1302	HA.6231	,,	34	
1303	HA.6232	,,	34	
1304	HA.6234	,,	34	

1305	HA.6235	"IM6"	34
1306	HA.6236	,,	34
1307	HA.6237	,,	34
1308	HA.6238	,,	34
1309	HA.6239	,,	34
1310	HA.6240	,,	34
1311	HA.6241	,,	34
1312	HA.6242	,,	34
1313	HA.6243	,,	34
1314	HA.6244	,,	34
1315	HA.6245	,,	34
1316	HA.7326	,,	34
1317	HA.7327	,,	34
1318	HA.7328	,,	34
1319	HA.7329	"REDD"	48
1320	HA.8247	"IM4"	34
1321	HA.8248	,,	34
1322	HA.8249	,,	34
1323	HA.8250	,,	34
1324	HA.8251	,,	34
1325	HA.8252	,,	34
1327	HA.8254	,,	34
1328	HA.8255	,,	34
1330	HA.8257	,,	34
1331	HA.8258	,,	34
1332	HA.8246	,,	34
1333	HA.8259	,,	34
1334	HA.8260	,,	34
1336	HA.8262	,,	34
1337	HA.8263	,,	34
1338	HA.8264	,,	34
1339	HA.8265	,,	34
1340	HA.8266	,,	34
1341	HA.8267	,,	34
1343	HA.8269	,,	34
1344	HA.8295	,,	34
1345	HA.8271	,,	34
1346	HA.8270	,,	34
1347	HA.8272	,,	34
1348	HA.8273	,,	34
1349	HA.8274	,,	34
1350	HA.8275	,,	34
1351	HA.8277	,,	34
1352	HA.8278	,,	34
1353	HA.8279	,,	34

Fleet Number	Registration Number	Type and Seating		Garage Number
1354	HA.8276	" IM4 "	34	
1355	HA.8280	,,	34	
1356	HA.8281	,,	34	
1357	HA.8284	,,	34	
1358	HA.8282	,,	34	
1359	HA.8283	,,	34	
1360	HA.8285	,,	34	
1361	HA.8286	,,	34	
1362	HA.8287	,,	34	
1363	HA.8288	,,	34	
1364	HA.8289	,,	34	
1365	HA.8290	,,	34	
1366	HA.8291	,,	34	
1367	HA.8292	,,	34	
1368	HA.8293	,,	34	
1369	HA.8294	,,	34	
1370	HA.8001	" REDD "	55	
1371	HA.8016	,,	55	
1372	HA.8026	,,	55	
1373	HA.8041	,,	55	
1375	HA.8003	,,	55	
1376	HA.8017	,,	55	
1377	HA.8004	,,	55	
1378	HA.8018	,,	55	
1379	HA.8019	,,	55	
1380	HA.8005	,,	55	
1381	HA.8027	,,	55	
1382	HA.8006	,,	55	
1383	HA.8020	,,	55	
1384	HA.8007	,,	55	
1385	HA.8021	,,	55	
1386	HA.8009	,,	55	
1387	HA.8008	,,	55	
1388	HA.8028	,,	55	
1389	HA.8010	,,	55	
1390	HA.8022	,,	55	
1391	HA.8048	,,	55	
1392	HA.8011	,,	55	
1393	HA.8012	,,	55	
1394	HA.8049	,,	55	
1395	HA.8029	,,	55	
1396	HA.8023	,,	55	

1928. "QL" type omnibus

Testing vehicle used for tree trimming and preparation of routes for double-deck omnibus operation. Note gauge in position on the roof

1929. "M" type single-deck omnibus, seating 34 passengers

193C. "RR" type long-distance saloon

1930. "MM" type 6-cylinder single-deck omnibus, seating 34 passengers

1930-3. "IM4" type single-deck omnibus, seating 34 passengers

1931-2. The first double-deck omnibus to be produced after 1922, designed with rear entrance

1397	HA.8030	" REDD "	55
1398	HA.8031	,,	55
1399	HA.8024	,,	55
1400	HA.8032	,,	55
1401	HA.8033	,,	55
1402	HA.8042	,,	55
1403	HA.8013	,,	55
1404	HA.8034	,,	55
1405	HA.8015	,,	55
1406	HA.8025	,,	55
1407	HA.8014	,,	55
1408	HA.8035	,,	55
1409	HA.8043	,,	55
1410	HA.8036	,,	55
1411	HA.8037	,,	55
1412	HA.8044	,,	55
1413	HA.8045	,,	55
1414	HA.8038	,,	55
1415	HA.8039	,,	55
1416	HA.8046	,,	55
1417	HA.8040	,,	55
1418	HA.8047	,,	55
1419	HA.8050	,,	55
1420	HA.8296	" IM6 "	34
1421	HA.8297	,,	34
1422	HA.8298	,,	34
1423	HA.8299	,,	34
1424	HA.8300	,,	34
1425	HA.8302	,,	34
1426	HA.8301	,,	34
1427	HA.8303	,,	34
1428	HA.8306	,,	34
1430	HA.8304	,,	34
1431	HA.8305	,,	34
1432	HA.8308	,,	34
1433	HA.8309	,,	34
1434	HA.8310	,,	34
1435	HA.8312	,,	34
1436	HA.8311	,,	34
1437	HA.8313	,,	34
1438	HA.8314	,,	34
1439	HA.8315	,,	34
1440	HA.8316	,,	34
1441	HA.8317	,,	34
1442	HA.8319	,,	34

Fleet Number	Registration Number	Type and Seating		Garage Number
1443	HA.8318	"IM6"	34	
1444	HA.8320	,,	34	
1445	HA.8321	,,	34	
1446	HA.8322	,,	34	
1447	HA.8323	,,	34	
1448	HA.9000	"FEDD"	52	
1449	HA.8324	"IM4"	34	
1450	HA.8325	,,	34	
1452	HA.8349	,,	34	
1453	HA.8350	,,	34	
1454	HA.8351	,,	34	
1456	HA.8353	,,	34	
1457	HA.8354	,,	34	
1458	HA.8357	,,	34	
1459	HA.8355	,,	34	
1461	HA.8356	,,	34	
1462	HA.9358	,,	34	
1465	HA.9362	,,	34	
1466	HA.9363	,,	34	
1467	HA.9364	,,	34	
1469	HA.9366	,,	34	
1470	HA.9367	,,	34	
1471	HA.9368	,,	34	
1472	HA.9369	,,	34	
1473	HA.9370	,,	34	
1474	HA.9371	,,	34	
1475	HA.9372	,,	34	
1476	HA.9373	,,	34	
1477	HA.9374	,,	34	
1478	HA.9375	,,	34	
1479	HA.9376	"BRR"	34	
1480	HA.9377	,,	34	
1481	HA.9378	,,	34	
1482	HA.9379	,,	34	
1483	HA.9380	,,	34	
1484	HA.9381	,,	34	
1485	HA.9382	,,	34	
1486	HA.9383	,,	34	
1487	HA.9384	,,	34	
1488	HA.9385	,,	34	
1489	HA.9386	,,	34	
1490	HA.9387	,,	34	

1491	HA.9388	" BRR "	34
1492	HA.9389	,,	34
1493	HA.9390	,,	34
1494	HA.9391	,,	34
1495	HA.9392	,,	34
1496	HA.9393	,,	34
1497	HA.9394	,,	34
1498	HA.9395	,,	34
1499	HA.9051	" LRR "	34
1500	HA.9451	" CON "	38
1501	HA.9452	,,	38
1502	HA.9453	,,	38
1503	HA.9454	,,	38
1504	HA.9455	,,	38
1505	HA.9456	,,	38
1506	HA.9457	,,	38
1507	HA.9460	,,	38
1508	HA.9458	,,	38
1509	HA.9459	,,	38
1510	HA.9461	,,	38
1511	HA.9462	,,	38
1512	HA.9463	,,	38
1513	HA.9464	,,	38
1514	HA.9465	,,	38
1515	HA.9466	,,	38
1516	HA.9467	,,	38
1517	HA.9468	,,	38
1518	HA.9469	,,	38
1519	HA.9470	,,	38
1520	HA.9471	,,	38
1521	HA.9472	,,	38
1522	HA.9473	,,	38
1523	HA.9474	,,	38
1524	HA.9475	,,	38
1525	HA.9476	,,	38
1526	HA.9477	,,	38
1527	HA.9478	,,	38
1528	HA.9479	,,	38
1529	HA.9480	,,	38
1530	HA.9481	" DON "	36
1531	HA.9482	" CON "	38
1532	HA.9483	,,	38
1533	HA.9484	" ON "	38
1534	HA.9485	" DON "	36
1535	HA.9486	" ON "	38

Fleet Number	Registration Number	Type and Seating	Garage Number
1536	HA.9401	" FEDD " 56	
1537	HA.9402	,, 56	
1538	HA.9403	,, 56	
1539	HA.9404	,, 56	
1540	HA.9405	,, 56	
1541	HA.9406	,, 56	
1542	HA.9407	,, 56	
1543	HA.9408	,, 56	
1544	HA.9409	,, 56	
1545	HA.9410	,, 56	
1546	HA.9411	,, 56	
1547	HA.9412	,, 56	
1548	HA.9422	,, 56	
1549	HA.9415	,, 56	
1550	HA.9416	,, 56	
1551	HA.9413	,, 56	
1552	HA.9414	,, 56	
1553	HA.9417	,, 56	
1554	HA.9418	,, 56	
1555	HA.9419	,, 56	
1556	HA.9420	,, 56	
1557	HA.9421	,, 56	
1558	HA.9423	,, 56	
1559	HA.9424	,, 56	
1560	HA.9425	,, 56	
1561	HA.9426	,, 56	
1562	HA.9427	,, 56	
1563	HA.9428	,, 56	
1564	HA.9429	,, 56	
1565	HA.9430	,, 56	
1566	HA.9431	,, 56	
1567	HA.9432	,, 56	
1568	HA.9433	,, 56	
1569	HA.9434	,, 56	
1570	HA.9436	,, 56	
1571	HA.9435	,, 56	
1572	HA.9437	,, 56	
1573	HA.9438	,, 56	
1574	HA.9439	,, 56	
1575	HA.9440	,, 56	
1576	HA.9441	,, 56	
1577	HA.9442	,, 56	

1578	HA.9443	" FEDD "	56
1579	HA.9444	,,	56
1580	HA.9445	,,	56
1581	HA.9446	,,	56
1582	HA.9447	,,	56
1583	HA.9448	,,	56
1584	HA.9449	,,	56
1585	HA.9450	,,	56
1586	HA.9396	" LRR "	34
1587	HA.9397	,,	34
1588	HA.9398	,,	34
1589	HA.9399	,,	34
1590	HA.9400	,,	34
1591	BHA.1	" S.1 "	40
1592	AHA.487	" ON "	38
1593	AHA.488	,,	38
1594	AHA.489	,,	38
1595	AHA.490	" CON "	38
1596	AHA.491	" ON "	38
1597	AHA.492	,,	38
1598	AHA.493	,,	38
1599	AHA.494	,,	38
1600	AHA.495	,,	38
1601	AHA.496	,,	38
1602	AHA.497	" CON "	38
1603	AHA.498	" ON "	38
1604	AHA.499	,,	38
1605	AHA.500	,,	38
1606	AHA.501	,,	38
1607	AHA.502	,,	38
1608	AHA.503	,,	38
1609	AHA.504	,,	38
1610	AHA.505	,,	38
1611	AHA.506	,,	38
1612	AHA.507	,,	38
1613	AHA.508	" CON "	38
1614	AHA.509	" ON "	38
1615	AHA.510	,,	38
1616	AHA.511	,,	38
1617	AHA.512	,,	38
1618	AHA.513	" CON "	38
1619	AHA.514	,,	38
1620	AHA.515	" ON "	38
1621	AHA.516	" CON "	38
1622	AHA.519	" ON "	38

Fleet Number	Registration Number	Type and Seating	Garage Number
1623	AHA.517	"ON" 38	
1624	AHA.518	"CON" 38	
1625	AHA.520	,, 38	
1626	AHA.521	,, 38	
1627	AHA.522	"ON" 38	
1628	AHA.523	,, 38	
1629	AHA.524	"CON" 38	
1630	AHA.525	"ON" 38	
1631	AHA.526	,, 38	
1632	AHA.527	"CON" 38	
1633	AHA.528	"ON" 38	
1634	AHA.529	,, 38	
1635	AHA.530	,, 38	
1636	AHA.531	,, 38	
1637	AHA.532	,, 38	
1638	AHA.533	,, 38	
1639	AHA.534	"CON" 38	
1640	AHA.535	"ON" 38	
1641	AHA.536	,, 38	
1642	AHA.587	"LRR" 34	
1643	AHA.588	,, 34	
1644	AHA.589	,, 34	
1645	AHA.590	,, 34	
1646	AHA.591	,, 34	
1647	AHA.592	,, 34	
1648	AHA.593	,, 34	
1649	AHA.594	,, 34	
1650	AHA.595	,, 34	
1651	AHA.596	,, 34	
1652	AHA.597	,, 34	
1653	AHA.598	,, 34	
1654	AHA.599	,, 34	
1655	AHA.600	,, 34	
1656	AHA.601	,, 34	
1657	AHA.602	,, 34	
1658	AHA.603	,, 34	
1659	AHA.604	,, 34	
1660	AHA.605	,, 34	
1661	AHA.606	,, 34	
1662	AHA.607	,, 34	
1663	AHA.608	,, 34	
1664	AHA.609	,, 34	

1665	AHA.610	" LRR "	34
1666	AHA.611	,,	34
1667	AHA.621	" OLR "	34
1668	AHA.612	,,	34
1669	AHA.613	,,	34
1670	AHA.614	,,	34
1671	AHA.615	,,	34
1672	AHA.616	,,	34
1673	AHA.617	,,	34
1674	AHA.618	,,	34
1675	AHA.619	,,	34
1676	AHA.620	,,	34
1677	AHA.622	,,	34
1678	AHA.623	,,	34
1679	AHA.624	,,	34
1680	AHA.625	,,	34
1681	AHA.626	,,	34
1682	AHA.627	,,	34
1683	AHA.628	,,	34
1684	AHA.629	,,	34
1685	AHA.630	,,	34
1686	AHA.631	,,	34
1687	AHA.632	,,	34
1688	AHA.633	,,	34
1689	AHA.634	,,	34
1690	AHA.635	,,	34
1691	AHA.636	,,	34
1692	AHA.577	" DON "	36
1693	AHA.578	,,	36
1694	AHA.579	,,	36
1695	AHA.580	,,	36
1696	AHA.537	,,	36
1697	AHA.581	,,	36
1698	AHA.583	,,	36
1699	AHA.584	,,	36
1700	AHA.585	,,	36
1701	AHA.586	,,	36
1702	AHA.538	,,	36
1703	AHA.582	,,	36
1704	AHA.539	,,	36
1705	AHA.540	,,	36
1706	AHA.541	,,	36
1707	AHA.542	,,	36
1708	AHA.543	,,	36
1709	AHA.544	,,	36

Fleet Number	Registration Number	Type and Seating	Garage Number
1710	AHA.545	"DON" 36	
1711	AHA.546	,, 36	
1712	AHA.547	,, 36	
1713	AHA.548	,, 36	
1714	AHA.549	,, 36	
1715	AHA.550	,, 36	
1716	AHA.551	,, 36	
1717	AHA.552	,, 36	
1718	AHA.553	,, 36	
1719	AHA.554	,, 36	
1720	AHA.555	,, 36	
1621	AHA.556	,, 36	
1722	AHA.557	,, 36	
1723	AHA.558	,, 36	
1724	AHA.559	,, 36	
1725	AHA.560	,, 36	
1726	AHA.561	,, 36	
1727	AHA.562	,, 36	
1728	AHA.563	,, 36	
1729	AHA.564	,, 36	
1730	AHA.565	,, 36	
1731	AHA.566	,, 36	
1732	AHA.567	,, 36	
1733	AHA.568	,, 36	
1734	AHA.569	,, 36	
1735	AHA.570	,, 36	
1736	AHA.571	,, 36	
1737	AHA.572	,, 36	
1738	AHA.573	,, 36	
1739	AHA.574	,, 36	
1740	AHA.575	,, 36	
1741	AHA.576	"ON" 38	
1742	BHA.303	"FEDD" 56	
1743	BHA.302	,, 56	
1744	BHA.301	,, 56	
1745	BHA.304	,, 56	
1746	BHA.305	,, 56	
1747	BHA.306	,, 56	
1748	BHA.307	,, 56	
1749	BHA.371	,, 56	
1750	BHA.308	,, 56	
1751	BHA.309	,, 56	

1752	BHA.310	"FEDD"	56
1753	BHA.311	,,	56
1754	BHA.312	,,	56
1755	BHA.313	,,	56
1756	BHA.314	,,	56
1757	BHA.315	,,	56
1758	BHA.316	,,	56
1759	BHA.372	,,	56
1760	BHA.317	,,	56
1761	BHA.318	,,	56
1762	BHA.319	,,	56
1763	BHA.320	,,	56
1764	BHA.321	,,	56
1765	BHA.322	,,	56
1766	BHA.323	,,	56
1767	BHA.324	,,	56
1768	BHA.325	,,	56
1769	BHA.373	,,	56
1770	BHA.374	,,	56
1771	BHA.326	,,	56
1772	BHA.327	,,	56
1773	BHA.328	,,	56
1774	BHA.329	,,	56
1775	BHA.330	,,	56
1776	BHA.375	,,	56
1777	BHA.376	,,	56
1778	BHA.377	,,	56
1779	BHA.378	,,	56
1780	BHA.331	,,	56
1781	BHA.379	,,	56
1782	BHA.380	,,	56
1783	BHA.381	,,	56
1784	BHA.382	,,	56
1785	BHA.383	,,	56
1786	BHA.384	,,	56
1787	BHA.385	,,	56
1788	BHA.332	,,	56
1789	BHA.333	,,	56
1790	BHA.334	,,	56
1791	BHA.335	,,	56
1792	BHA.336	,,	56
1793	BHA.337	,,	56
1794	BHA.338	,,	56
1795	BHA.339	,,	56
1796	BHA.340	,,	56

Fleet Number	Registration Number	Type and Seating	Garage Number
1797	BHA.341	" FEDD " 56	
1798	BHA.342	,, 56	
1799	BHA.343	,, 56	
1800	BHA.344	,, 56	
1801	BHA.345	,, 56	
1802	BHA.346	,, 56	
1803	BHA.347	,, 56	
1804	BHA.348	,, 56	
1805	BHA.349	,, 56	
1806	BHA.350	,, 56	
1807	BHA.351	,, 56	
1808	BHA.352	,, 56	
1809	BHA.353	,, 56	
1810	BHA.354	,, 56	
1811	BHA.355	,, 56	
1812	BHA.356	,, 56	
1813	BHA.357	,, 56	
1814	BHA.358	,, 56	
1815	BHA.359	,, 56	
1816	BHA.360	,, 56	
1817	BHA.361	,, 56	
1818	BHA.362	,, 56	
1819	BHA.363	,, 56	
1820	BHA.364	,, 56	
1821	BHA.365	,, 56	
1822	BHA.366	,, 56	
1823	BHA.367	,, 56	
1824	BHA.368	,, 56	
1825	BHA.369	,, 56	
1826	BHA.370	,, 56	
1827	BHA.386	,, 56	
1828	BHA.387	,, 56	
1829	BHA.388	,, 56	
1830	BHA.389	,, 56	
1831	BHA.390	,, 56	
1832	BHA.391	,, 56	
1833	BHA.392	,, 56	
1834	BHA.393	,, 56	
1835	BHA.394	,, 56	
1836	BHA.395	,, 56	
1837	BHA.396	,, 56	
1838	BHA.397	,, 56	

1839	BHA.398	" FEDD "	56
1840	BHA.399	,,	56
1841	BHA.400	,,	56
1842	BHA.801	,,	56
1843	BHA.802	,,	56
1844	BHA.803	,,	56
1845	BHA.804	,,	56
1846	BHA.805	,,	56
1847	BHA.806	,,	56
1848	BHA.807	,,	56
1849	BHA.808	,,	56
1850	BHA.809	,,	56
1851	BHA.810	,,	56
1852	BHA.811	,,	56
1853	BHA.812	,,	56
1854	BHA.813	,,	56
1855	BHA.814	,,	56
1856	BHA.815	,,	56
1857	BHA.816	,,	56
1858	BHA.817	,,	56
1859	BHA.818	,,	56
1860	BHA.819	,,	56
1861	BHA.820	,,	56
1862	BHA.821	,,	56
1863	BHA.822	,,	56
1864	BHA.823	,,	56
1865	BHA.824	,,	56
1866	BHA.825	,,	56
1867	BHA.826	,,	56
1868	BHA.827	,,	56
1869	BHA.828	,,	56
1870	BHA.829	,,	56
1871	BHA.830	,,	56
1872	BHA.831	,,	56
1873	BHA.832	,,	56
1874	BHA.833	,,	56
1875	BHA.834	,,	56
1876	BHA.835	,,	56
1877	CHA.501	" SON "	39
1878	CHA.502	,,	39
1879	CHA.503	,,	39
1880	CHA.504	,,	39
1881	CHA.505	,,	39
1882	CHA.506	,,	39
1883	CHA.507	,,	39

Fleet Number	Registration Number	Type and Seating		Garage Number
1884	CHA.508	"SON"	39	
1885	CHA.509	,,	39	
1886	CHA.510	,,	39	
1887	CHA.511	,,	39	
1888	CHA.512	,,	39	
1889	CHA.513	,,	39	
1890	CHA.514	,,	39	
1891	CHA.515	,,	39	
1892	CHA.516	,,	39	
1893	CHA.517	,,	39	
1894	CHA.518	,,	39	
1895	CHA.519	,,	39	
1896	CHA.520	,,	39	
1897	CHA.521	,,	39	
1898	CHA.522	,,	39	
1899	CHA.523	,,	39	
1900	CHA.524	,,	39	
1901	CHA.525	,,	39	
1902	CHA.526	,,	39	
1903	CHA.527	,,	39	
1904	CHA.528	,,	39	
1905	CHA.529	,,	39	
1906	CHA.530	,,	39	
1907	CHA.531	,,	39	
1908	CHA.532	,,	39	
1909	CHA.533	,,	39	
1910	CHA.534	,,	39	
1911	CHA.535	,,	39	
1912	CHA.536	,,	39	
1913	CHA.537	,,	39	
1914	CHA.538	,,	39	
1915	CHA.539	,,	39	
1916	CHA.540	,,	39	
1917	CHA.541	,,	39	
1918	CHA.542	,,	39	
1919	CHA.543	,,	39	
1920	CHA.544	,,	39	
1921	CHA.545	,,	39	
1922	CHA.546	,,	39	
1923	CHA.547	,,	39	
1924	CHA.548	,,	39	
1925	CHA.549	,,	39	

1926	CHA.550	" SON "	39
1927	CHA.551	,,	39
1928	CHA.552	,,	39
1929	CHA.553	,,	39
1930	CHA.554	,,	39
1931	CHA.555	,,	39
1932	CHA.556	,,	39
1933	CHA.557	,,	39
1934	CHA.558	,,	39
1935	CHA.559	,,	39
1936	CHA.560	,,	39
1937	CHA.561	,,	39
1938	CHA.562	,,	39
1939	CHA.563	,,	39
1940	CHA.564	,,	39
1941	CHA.565	,,	39
1942	CHA.1	" S.2 "	40
1943	CHA.2	" S.3 "	40
1944	CHA.3	" S.4 "	40
1968	CHA.950	" SLR "	30
1969	CHA.951	,,	30
1970	CHA.952	,,	30
1971	CHA.953	,,	30
1972	CHA.954	,,	30
1973	CHA.955	,,	30
1974	CHA.956	,,	30
1975	CHA.957	,,	30
1976	CHA.958	,,	30
1977	CHA.959	,,	30
1978	CHA.960	,,	30
1979	CHA.961	,,	30
1980	CHA.962	,,	30
1981	CHA.963	,,	30
1982	CHA.964	,,	30
1983	CHA.965	,,	30
1984	CHA.966	,,	30
1985	CHA.967	,,	30
1986	CHA.968	,,	30
1987	CHA.969	,,	30
1988	CHA.970	,,	30
1989	CHA.971	,,	30
1990	CHA.972	,,	30
1991	CHA.973	,,	30
1992	CHA.974	,,	30
1993	CHA.975	,,	30

Fleet Number	Registration Number	Type and Seating	Garage Number
1994	CHA.976	" SLR " 30	
1995	CHA.977	,, 30	
1996	CHA.978	,, 30	
1997	CHA.979	,, 30	
1998	CHA.980	,, 30	
1999	CHA.981	,, 30	
2000	CHA.982	,, 30	
2001	CHA.983	,, 30	
2002	CHA.984	,, 30	
2003	CHA.985	,, 30	
2004	CHA.986	,, 30	
2005	CHA.987	,, 30	
2006	CHA.988	,, 30	
2007	CHA.989	,, 30	
2008	CHA.990	,, 30	
2009	CHA.991	,, 30	
2010	CHA.992	,, 30	
2011	CHA.993	,, 30	
2012	CHA.994	,, 30	
2013	CHA.995	,, 30	
2014	CHA.996	,, 30	
2015	CHA.997	,, 30	
2016	CHA.998	,, 30	
2017	CHA.999	,, 30	
2019	DHA.637	" SON " 38	
2020	DHA.638	,, 38	
2021	DHA.639	,, 38	
2022	DHA.640	,, 38	
2023	DHA.641	,, 38	
2024	DHA.642	,, 38	
2025	DHA.643	,, 38	
2026	DHA.644	,, 38	
2027	DHA.645	,, 38	
2028	DHA.646	,, 38	
2029	DHA.647	,, 38	
2030	DHA.648	,, 38	
2031	DHA.649	,, 38	
2032	DHA.650	,, 38	
2033	DHA.651	,, 38	
2034	DHA.652	,, 38	
2035	DHA.653	,, 38	
2036	DHA.654	,, 38	

2037	DHA.655	" SON "	38
2038	DHA.656	,,	38
2039	DHA.657	,,	38
2040	DHA.658	,,	38
2041	DHA.659	,,	38
2042	DHA.660	,,	38
2043	DHA.661	,,	38
2044	DHA.662	,,	38
2045	DHA.663	,,	38
2046	DHA.664	,,	38
2047	DHA.665	,,	38
2048	DHA.666	,,	38
2049	DHA.667	,,	38
2050	DHA.668	,,	38
2051	DHA.669	,,	38
2052	DHA.670	,,	38
2053	DHA.671	,,	38
2054	DHA.672	,,	38
2055	DHA.673	,,	38
2056	DHA.674	,,	38
2057	DHA.675	,,	38
2058	DHA.676	,,	38
2059	DHA.677	,,	38
2060	DHA.678	,,	38
2061	DHA.679	,,	38
2062	DHA.680	,,	38
2063	DHA.681	,,	38
2064	DHA.682	,,	38
2065	DHA.683	,,	38
2066	DHA.684	,,	38
2067	DHA.685	,,	38
2068	DHA.686	,,	38
2069	DHA.687	,,	38
2070	DHA.688	,,	38
2071	DHA.689	,,	38
2072	DHA.690	,,	38
2073	DHA.691	,,	38
2074	DHA.692	,,	38
2075	DHA.693	,,	38
2076	DHA.694	,,	38
2077	DHA.695	,,	38
2078	DHA.696	,,	38
2079	DHA.697	,,	38
2080	DHA.698	,,	38
2081	DHA.699	,,	38

Fleet Number	Registration Number	Type and Seating		Garage Number
2082	DHA.700	" SON "	38	
2083	DHA.701	,,	38	
2084	DHA.702	,,	38	
2085	DHA.703	,,	38	
2086	DHA.704	,,	38	
2087	DHA.705	,,	38	
2088	DHA.706	,,	38	
2089	DHA.707	,,	38	
2090	DHA.708	,,	38	
2091	DHA.709	,,	38	
2092	DHA.710	,,	38	
2093	DHA.711	,,	38	
2094	DHA.712	,,	38	
2095	DHA.713	,,	38	
2096	DHA.714	,,	38	
2097	DHA.715	,,	38	
2098	DHA.716	,,	38	
2099	DHA.717	,,	38	
2100	DHA.718	,,	38	
2101	DHA.719	,,	38	
2102	DHA.720	,,	38	
2103	DHA.721	,,	38	
2104	DHA.722	,,	38	
2105	DHA.723	,,	38	
2106	DHA.724	,,	38	
2107	DHA.725	,,	38	
2108	DHA.726	,,	38	
2109	DHA.727	,,	38	
2110	DHA.728	,,	38	
2111	DHA.729	,,	38	
2112	DHA.730	,,	38	
2113	DHA.731	,,	38	
2114	DHA.732	,,	38	
2115	DHA.733	,,	38	
2116	DHA.734	,,	38	
2117	DHA.735	,,	38	
2118	DHA.736	,,	38	
2119	EHA.251	" FEDD "	56	
2120	EHA.252	,,	56	
2121	EHA.253	,,	56	
2122	EHA.254	,,	56	
2123	EHA.255	,,	56	

1933. Front-entrance double-deck omnibus. This type was the standard production design in the years 1934-6 (with improved frontal appearance)

1934. "SON" type 38-seater single-deck omnibus, evolved from the "ON" petrol-engined type. This design became the standard single-deck type during the period 1936-9. Its variants were the "DON" type (Diesel-engined "ON"), produced in 1935, and the "CON," produced in 1935-6 and designed to run on heavy oil

1938. Experimental rear-engined omnibus, type "BHA.1." This vehicle was afterwards rebuilt with an under-floor engine, an arrangement since adopted as standard for all Midland "Red" single-deck vehicles

2124	EHA.256	"FEDD" 56
2125	EHA.257	,, 56
2126	EHA.258	,, 56
2127	EHA.259	,, 56
2128	EHA.260	,, 56
2129	EHA.261	,, 56
2130	EHA.262	,, 56
2131	EHA.263	,, 56
2132	EHA.264	,, 56
2133	EHA.265	,, 56
2134	EHA.266	,, 56
2135	EHA.267	,, 56
2136	EHA.268	,, 56
2137	EHA.269	,, 56
2138	EHA.270	,, 56
2139	EHA.271	,, 56
2140	EHA.272	,, 56
2141	EHA.273	,, 56
2142	EHA.274	,, 56
2143	EHA.275	,, 56
2144	EHA.276	,, 56
2145	EHA.277	,, 56
2146	EHA.278	,, 56
2147	EHA.279	,, 56
2148	EHA.280	,, 56
2149	EHA.281	,, 56
2150	EHA.282	,, 56
2151	EHA.283	,, 56
2152	EHA.284	,, 56
2153	EHA.285	,, 56
2154	EHA.286	,, 56
2155	EHA.287	,, 56
2156	EHA.288	,, 56
2157	EHA.289	,, 56
2158	EHA.290	,, 56
2159	EHA.291	,, 56
2160	EHA.292	,, 56
2161	EHA.293	,, 56
2162	EHA.294	,, 56
2163	EHA.295	,, 56
2164	EHA.296	,, 56
2165	EHA.297	,, 56
2166	EHA.298	,, 56
2167	EHA.299	,, 56
2168	EHA.300	,, 56

Fleet Number	Registration Number	Type and Seating		Garage Number
2169	EHA.737	" SON "	38	
2170	EHA.738	,,	38	
2171	EHA.739	,,	38	
2172	EHA.740	,,	38	
2173	EHA.741	,,	38	
2174	EHA.742	,,	38	
2175	EHA.743	,,	38	
2176	EHA.744	,,	38	
2177	EHA.745	,,	38	
2178	EHA.746	,,	38	
2179	EHA.747	,,	38	
2180	EHA.748	,,	38	
2181	EHA.749	,,	38	
2182	EHA.750	,,	38	
2183	EHA.751	,,	38	
2184	EHA.752	,,	38	
2185	EHA.753	,,	38	
2186	EHA.754	,,	38	
2187	EHA.755	,,	38	
2188	EHA.756	,,	38	
2189	EHA.757	,,	38	
2190	EHA.758	,,	38	
2191	EHA.759	,,	38	
2192	EHA.760	,,	38	
2193	EHA.761	,,	38	
2194	EHA.762	,,	38	
2195	EHA.763	,,	38	
2196	EHA.764	,,	38	
2197	EHA.765	,,	38	
2198	EHA.766	,,	38	
2199	EHA.767	,,	38	
2200	EHA.768	,,	38	
2201	EHA.769	,,	38	
2202	EHA.770	,,	38	
2203	EHA.771	,,	38	
2204	EHA.772	,,	38	
2205	EHA.773	,,	38	
2206	EHA.774	,,	38	
2207	EHA.775	,,	38	
2208	EHA.786	,,	38	
2209	EHA.777	,,	38	
2210	EHA.778	,,	38	

2211	EHA.779	" SON "	38
2212	EHA.780	,,	38
2213	EHA.781	,,	38
2214	EHA.782	,,	38
2215	EHA.783	,,	38
2216	EHA.784	,,	38
2217	EHA.785	,,	38
2218	EHA.776	,,	38
2219	FHA.201	" FEDD "	56
2220	FHA.202	,,	56
2221	FHA.203	,,	56
2222	FHA.204	,,	56
2223	FHA.205	,,	56
2224	FHA.206	,,	56
2225	FHA.207	,,	56
2226	FHA.208	,,	56
2227	FHA.209	,,	56
2228	FHA.210	,,	56
2229	FHA.211	,,	56
2230	FHA.212	,,	56
2231	FHA.213	,,	56
2232	FHA.214	,,	56
2233	FHA.215	,,	56
2234	FHA.216	,,	56
2235	FHA.217	,,	56
2236	FHA.218	,,	56
2237	FHA.219	,,	56
2238	FHA.220	,,	56
2239	FHA.221	,,	56
2240	FHA.200	,,	56
2241	FHA.223	,,	56
2242	FHA.224	,,	56
2243	FHA.225	,,	56
2244	FHA.226	,,	56
2245	FHA.227	,,	56
2246	FHA.228	,,	56
2247	FHA.229	,,	56
2248	FHA.230	,,	56
2249	FHA.231	,,	56
2250	FHA.232	,,	56
2251	FHA.233	,,	56
2252	FHA.234	,,	56
2253	FHA.235	,,	56
2254	FHA.236	,,	56
2255	FHA.237	,,	56

Fleet Number	Registration Number	Type and Seating	Garage Number
2256	FHA.238	" FEDD " 56	
2257	FHA.239	,, 56	
2258	FHA.240	,, 56	
2259	FHA.241	,, 56	
2260	FHA.242	,, 56	
2261	FHA.243	,, 56	
2262	FHA.244	,, 56	
2263	FHA.245	,, 56	
2264	FHA.246	,, 56	
2265	FHA.247	,, 56	
2266	FHA.248	,, 56	
2267	FHA.249	,, 56	
2268	FHA.250	,, 56	
2269	FHA.401	" ONC " 30	
2270	FHA.402	,, 30	
2271	FHA.403	,, 30	
2272	FHA.404	,, 30	
2273	FHA.405	,, 30	
2274	FHA.406	,, 30	
2275	FHA.407	,, 30	
2276	FHA.408	,, 30	
2277	FHA.409	,, 30	
2278	FHA.410	,, 30	
2279	FHA.411	,, 30	
2280	FHA.412	,, 30	
2281	FHA.413	,, 30	
2282	FHA.414	,, 30	
2283	FHA.415	,, 30	
2284	FHA.416	,, 30	
2285	FHA.417	,, 30	
2286	FHA.418	,, 30	
2287	FHA.419	,, 30	
2288	FHA.420	,, 30	
2289	FHA.421	,, 30	
2290	FHA.422	,, 30	
2291	FHA.423	,, 30	
2292	FHA.424	,, 30	
2293	FHA.425	,, 30	
2294	FHA.449	" SON " 38	
2295	FHA.450	,, 38	
2296	FHA.451	,, 38	
2297	FHA.452	,, 38	

2298	FHA.453	" SON "	38
2299	FHA.454	,,	38
2300	FHA.455	,,	38
2301	FHA.456	,,	38
2302	FHA.457	,,	38
2303	FHA.458	,,	38
2304	FHA.459	,,	38
2305	FHA.460	,,	38
2306	FHA.461	,,	38
2307	FHA.462	,,	38
2308	FHA.463	,,	38
2309	FHA.464	,,	38
2310	FHA.465	,,	38
2311	FHA.466	,,	38
2312	FHA.467	,,	38
2313	FHA.468	,,	38
2314	FHA.469	,,	38
2315	FHA.470	,,	38
2316	FHA.471	,,	38
2317	FHA.472	,,	38
2318	FHA.473	,,	38
2319	FHA.474	,,	38
2320	FHA.475	,,	38
2321	FHA.476	,,	38
2322	FHA.477	,,	38
2323	FHA.478	,,	38
2324	FHA.479	,,	38
2325	FHA.480	,,	38
2326	FHA.481	,,	38
2327	FHA.482	,,	38
2328	FHA.483	,,	38
2329	FHA.484	,,	38
2330	FHA.485	,,	38
2331	FHA.486	,,	38
2332	FHA.836	" FEDD "	56
2333	FHA.837	,,	56
2334	FHA.838	,,	56
2335	FHA.839	,,	56
2336	FHA.840	,,	56
2337	FHA.841	,,	56
2338	FHA.842	,,	56
2339	FHA.843	,,	56
2340	FHA.844	,,	56
2341	FHA.845	,,	56
2342	FHA.846	,,	56

Fleet Number	Registration Number	Type and Seating	Garage Number
2343	FHA.847	"FEDD" 56	
2344	FHA.848	,, 56	
2345	FHA.849	,, 56	
2346	FHA.850	,, 56	
2347	FHA.851	,, 56	
2348	FHA.852	,, 56	
2349	FHA.853	,, 56	
2350	FHA.854	,, 56	
2351	FHA.855	,, 56	
2352	FHA.856	,, 56	
2353	FHA.857	,, 56	
2354	FHA.858	,, 56	
2355	FHA.859	,, 56	
2356	FHA.860	,, 56	
2357	FHA.861	,, 56	
2358	FHA.862	,, 56	
2359	FHA.863	,, 56	
2360	FHA.864	,, 56	
2361	FHA.865	,, 56	
2362	FHA.866	,, 56	
2363	FHA.867	,, 56	
2364	FHA.868	,, 56	
2365	FHA.869	,, 56	
2366	FHA.870	,, 56	
2367	FHA.871	,, 56	
2368	FHA.872	,, 56	
2369	FHA.873	,, 56	
2370	FHA.874	,, 56	
2371	FHA.875	,, 56	
2372	FHA.876	,, 56	
2373	FHA.877	,, 56	
2374	FHA.878	,, 56	
2375	FHA.879	,, 56	
2376	FHA.880	,, 56	
2377	FHA.881	,, 56	
2378	FHA.882	,, 56	
2379	FHA.883	,, 56	
2380	FHA.884	,, 56	
2381	FHA.885	,, 56	
2382	GHA.301	"SON" 38	
2383	GHA.302	,, 38	
2384	GHA.303	,, 38	

2385	GHA.304	"SON"	38
2386	GHA.305	,,	38
2387	GHA.306	,,	38
2388	GHA.307	,,	38
2389	GHA.308	,,	38
2390	GHA.309	,,	38
2391	GHA.310	,,	38
2392	GHA.311	,,	38
2393	GHA.312	,,	38
2394	GHA.313	,,	38
2395	GHA.314	,,	38
2396	GHA.315	,,	38
2397	GHA.316	,,	38
2398	GHA.317	,,	38
2399	GHA.318	,,	38
2400	GHA.319	,,	38
2401	GHA.320	,,	38
2402	GHA.321	,,	38
2403	GHA.322	,,	38
2404	GHA.323	,,	38
2405	GHA.324	,,	38
2406	GHA.325	,,	38
2407	GHA.326	,,	38
2408	GHA.327	,,	38
2409	GHA.328	,,	38
2410	GHA.329	,,	38
2411	GHA.330	,,	38
2412	GHA.331	,,	38
2413	GHA.332	,,	38
2414	GHA.333	,,	38
2415	GHA.334	,,	38
2416	GHA.335	,,	38
2417	GHA.336	,,	38
2418	GHA.337	,,	38
2419	GHA.338	,,	38
2420	GHA.339	,,	38
2421	GHA.340	,,	38
2422	GHA.341	,,	38
2423	GHA.342	,,	38
2424	GHA.343	,,	38
2425	GHA.344	,,	38
2426	GHA.345	,,	38
2427	GHA.346	,,	38
2428	GHA.347	"SON"	38
2429	GHA.348	,,	38

Fleet Number	Registration Number	Type and Seating		Garage Number
3037	HHA.638	"S.6"	40	
3038	HHA.639	,,	40	
3039	HHA.640	,,	40	
3040	HHA.641	,,	40	
3041	HHA.642	,,	40	
3042	HHA.643	,,	40	
3043	HHA.644	,,	40	
3044	HHA.645	,,	40	
3045	HHA.646	,,	40	
3046	HHA.647	,,	40	
3047	HHA.648	,,	40	
3048	HHA.649	,,	40	
3049	HHA.650	,,	40	
3050	HHA.651	,,	40	
3051	HHA.652	,,	40	
3052	HHA.653	,,	40	
3053	HHA.654	,,	40	
3054	HHA.655	,,	40	
3055	HHA.656	,,	40	
3056	HHA.657	,,	40	
3057	HHA.658	,,	40	
3058	HHA.659	,,	40	
3059	HHA.660	,,	40	
3060	HHA.661	,,	40	
3061	HHA.662	,,	40	
3062	HHA.663	,,	40	
3063	HHA.664	,,	40	
3064	HHA.665	,,	40	
3065	HHA.666	,,	40	
3066	HHA.667	,,	40	
3067	HHA.668	,,	40	
3068	HHA.669	,,	40	
3069	HHA.670	,,	40	
3070	HHA.671	,,	40	
3071	HHA.672	,,	40	
3072	HHA.673	,,	40	
3073	HHA.674	,,	40	
3074	HHA.675	,,	40	
3075	HHA.676	,,	40	
3076	HHA.677	,,	40	
3077	HHA.678	,,	40	
3078	HHA.679	,,	40	
3079	HHA.680	,,	40	

Prototype of post-war single-deck omnibus. This vehicle, which is equipped with an under-floor engine located amidships, seats 40 passengers. Three hundred of this type are on order

Interior of post-war single-deck omnibus, looking towards the driving seat

2493	RC.1291	"IM4"	34
2494	RC.1295	,,	34
2497	GHA.921	"REDD" Guy	56
2498	GHA.922	,,	56
2499	GHA.923	,,	56
2500	GHA.924	,,	56
2501	GHA.925	,,	56
2502	GHA.926	,,	56
2503	GHA.927	,,	56
2504	GHA.928	,,	56
2505	GHA.929	,,	56
2506	GHA.930	,,	56
2507	GHA.931	,,	56
2508	GHA.932	,,	56
2509	GHA.933	"REDD" Daimler	56
2510	GHA.934	,,	56
2511	GHA.935	,,	56
2512	GHA.936	,,	56
2513	GHA.937	,,	56
2514	GHA.938	,,	56
2515	GHA.939	,,	56
2516	GHA.940	,,	56
2517	GHA.941	,,	56
2518	GHA.942	,,	56
2519	GHA.943	,,	56
2520	GHA.944	,,	56
2521	GHA.945	,,	56
2522	GHA.946	,,	56
2530	GHA.965	,,	56
2531	GHA.966	,,	56
2532	GHA.967	,,	56
2533	GHA.968	,,	56
2534	GHA.969	,,	56
2535	GHA.970	,,	56
2536	GHA.971	,,	56
2537	GHA.972	,,	56
2538	GHA.973	,,	56
2539	GHA.974	,,	56
2540	GHA.975	,,	56
2541	HHA.1	1944 "D1" "REDD"	56
2542	GHA.992	"REDD" Daimler	56

Fleet Number	Registration Number	Type and Seating	Garage Number
		"REDD"	
2543	GHA.993	Daimler 56	
2544	GHA.994	,, 56	
2545	GHA.995	,, 56	
2546	GHA.996	,, 56	
2547	GHA.997	,, 56	
2548	GHA.998	,, 56	
2549	GHA.999	,, 56	
2550	HHA.2	"REDD"	
		Guy 56	
2551	HHA.3	,, 56	
2552	HHA.4	,, 56	
2553	HHA.5	,, 56	
2554	HHA.6	,, 56	
2555	HHA.7	,, 56	
2556	HHA.8	,, 56	
2557	HHA.9	,, 56	
2558	HHA.10	,, 56	
2559	HHA.11	,, 56	
2560	HHA.12	,, 56	
2561	HHA.13	,, 56	
2562	HHA.14	,, 56	
2563	HHA.15	,, 56	
2564	HHA.16	,, 56	
2565	HHA.17	,, 56	
2566	HHA.18	,, 56	
2567	HHA.19	,, 56	
2568	HHA.20	,, 56	
2569	HHA.21	,, 56	
2570	HHA.22	,, 56	
2571	HHA.23	,, 56	
2572	HHA.24	,, 56	
2573	HHA.25	,, 56	
2574	HHA.26	,, 56	
2575	HHA.27	,, 56	
2576	HHA.28	,, 56	
2577	HHA.29	,, 56	
2578	HHA.30	,, 56	
2579	HHA.222	"S.5" 40	
2580	HHA.57	"REDD"	
		Guy 56	
2581	HHA.58	,, 56	

2582	HHA.59	" REDD "	56
2583	HHA.60	Guy	56
2584	HHA.61	,,	56
2585	HHA.62	,,	56
2586	HHA.81	,,	56
2587	HHA.82	,,	56
2588	HHA.83	,,	56
2589	HHA.84	,,	56
2590	HHA.85	,,	56
3000	HHA.601	" S.6 "	40
3001	HHA.602	,,	40
3002	HHA.603	,,	40
3003	HHA.604	,,	40
3004	HHA.605	,,	40
3005	HHA.606	,,	40
3006	HHA.607	,,	40
3007	HHA.608	,,	40
3008	HHA.609	,,	40
3009	HHA.610	,,	40
3010	HHA.611	,,	40
3011	HHA.612	,,	40
3012	HHA.613	,,	40
3013	HHA.614	,,	40
3014	HHA.615	,,	40
3015	HHA.616	,,	40
3016	HHA.617	,,	40
3017	HHA.618	,,	40
3018	HHA.619	,,	40
3019	HHA.620	,,	40
3020	HHA.621	,,	40
3021	HHA.622	,,	40
3022	HHA.623	,,	40
3023	HHA.624	,,	40
3024	HHA.625	,,	40
3025	HHA.626	,,	40
3026	HHA.627	,,	40
3027	HHA.628	,,	40
3028	HHA.629	,,	40
3029	HHA.630	,,	40
3030	HHA.631	,,	40
3031	HHA.632	,,	40
3032	HHA.633	,,	40
3033	HHA.634	,,	40
3034	HHA.635	,,	40
3035	HHA.636	,,	40
3036	HHA.637	,,	40

3037-3079

Fleet Number	Registration Number	Type and Seating		Garage Number
3037	HHA.638	"S.6"	40	
3038	HHA.639	,,	40	
3039	HHA.640	,,	40	
3040	HHA.641	,,	40	
3041	HHA.642	,,	40	
3042	HHA.643	,,	40	
3043	HHA.644	,,	40	
3044	HHA.645	,,	40	
3045	HHA.646	,,	40	
3046	HHA.647	,,	40	
3047	HHA.648	,,	40	
3048	HHA.649	,,	40	
3049	HHA.650	,,	40	
3050	HHA.651	,,	40	
3051	HHA.652	,,	40	
3052	HHA.653	,,	40	
3053	HHA.654	,,	40	
3054	HHA.655	,,	40	
3055	HHA.656	,,	40	
3056	HHA.657	,,	40	
3057	HHA.658	,,	40	
3058	HHA.659	,,	40	
3059	HHA.660	,,	40	
3060	HHA.661	,,	40	
3061	HHA.662	,,	40	
3062	HHA.663	,,	40	
3063	HHA.664	,,	40	
3064	HHA.665	,,	40	
3065	HHA.666	,,	40	
3066	HHA.667	,,	40	
3067	HHA.668	,,	40	
3068	HHA.669	,,	40	
3069	HHA.670	,,	40	
3070	HHA.671	,,	40	
3071	HHA.672	,,	40	
3072	HHA.673	,,	40	
3073	HHA.674	,,	40	
3074	HHA.675	,,	40	
3075	HHA.676	,,	40	
3076	HHA.677	,,	40	
3077	HHA.678	,,	40	
3078	HHA.679	,,	40	
3079	HHA.680	,,	40	

3080	HHA.681	"S.6"	40
3081	HHA.682	,,	40
3082	HHA.683	,,	40
3083	HHA.684	,,	40
3084	HHA.685	,,	40
3085	HHA.686	,,	40
3086	HHA.687	,,	40
3087	HHA.688	,,	40
3088	HHA.689	,,	40
3089	HHA.690	,,	40
3090	HHA.691	,,	40
3091	HHA.692	,,	40
3092	HHA.693	,,	40
3093	HHA.694	,,	40
3094	HHA.695	,,	40
3095	HHA.696	,,	40
3096	HHA.697	,,	40
3097	HHA.698	,,	40
3098	HHA.699	,,	40
3099	HHA.700	,,	40
3100	JHA.1	"REDD" "AD2"	56
3101	JHA.2	,,	56
3102	JHA.3	,,	56
3103	JHA.4	,,	56
3104	JHA.5	,,	56
3105	JHA.6	,,	56
3106	JHA.7	,,	56
3107	JHA.8	,,	56
3108	JHA.9	,,	56
3109	JHA.10	,,	56
3110	JHA.11	,,	56
3111	JHA.12	,,	56
3112	JHA.13	,,	56
3113	JHA.14	,,	56
3114	JHA.15	,,	56
3115	JHA.16	,,	56
3116	JHA.17	,	56
3117	JHA.18	,,	56
3118	JHA.19	,,	56
3119	JHA.20	,,	56
3120	JHA.21	,,	56
3121	JHA.22	,,	56
3122	JHA.23	,,	56
3123	JHA.24	,,	56
3124	JHA.25	,,	56

Fleet Number	Registration Number	Type and Seating	Garage Number
3125	JHA.26	"REDD" 56	
3126	JHA.27	"AD2" 56	
3127	JHA.28	,, 56	
3128	JHA.29	,, 56	
3129	JHA.30	,, 56	
3130	JHA.31	,, 56	
3131	JHA.32	,, 56	
3132	JHA.33	,, 56	
3133	JHA.34	,, 56	
3134	JHA.35	,, 56	
3135	JHA.36	,, 56	
3136	JHA.37	,, 56	
3137	JHA.38	,, 56	
3138	JHA.39	,, 56	
3139	JHA.40	,, 56	
3140	JHA.41	,, 56	
3141	JHA.42	,, 56	
3142	JHA.43	,, 56	
3143	JHA.44	,, 56	
3144	JHA.45	,, 56	
3145	JHA.46	,, 56	
3146	JHA.47	,, 56	
3147	JHA.48	,, 56	
3148	JHA.49	,, 56	
3149	JHA.50	,, 56	
3150	JHA.51	,, 56	
3151	JHA.52	,, 56	
3152	JHA.53	,, 56	
3153	JHA.54	,, 56	
3154	JHA.55	,, 56	
3155	JHA.56	,, 56	
3156	JHA.57	,, 56	
3157	JHA.58	,, 56	
3158	JHA.59	,, 56	
3159	JHA.60	,, 56	
3160	JHA.61	,, 56	
3161	JHA.62	,, 56	
3162	JHA.63	,, 56	
3163	JHA.64	,, 56	
3164	JHA.65	,, 56	
3165	JHA.66	,, 56	
3166	JHA.67	,, 56	
3167	JHA.68	,, 56	

		" REDD "	
3168	JHA.69	" AD2 "	56
3169	JHA.70	,,	56
3170	JHA.71	,,	56
3171	JHA.72	,,	56
3172	JHA.73	,,	56
3173	JHA.74	,,	56
3174	JHA.75	,,	56
3175	JHA.76	,,	56
3176	JHA.77	,,	56
3177	JHA.78	,,	56
3178	JHA.79	,,	56
3179	JHA.80	,,	56
3180	JHA.81	,,	56
3181	JHA.82	,,	56
3182	JHA.83	,,	56
3183	JHA.84	,,	56
3184	JHA.85	,,	56
3185	JHA.86	,,	56
3186	JHA.87	,,	56
3187	JHA.88	,,	56
3188	JHA.89	,,	56
3189	JHA.90	,,	56
3190	JHA.91	,,	56
3191	JHA.92	,,	56
3192	JHA.93	,,	56
3193	JHA.94	,,	56
3194	JHA.95	,,	56
3195	JHA.96	,,	56
3196	JHA.97	,,	56
3197	JHA.98	,,	56
3198	JHA.99	,,	56
3199	JHA.100	,,	56
3200	JHA.800	" S.8 "	40
3201	JHA.801	,,	40
3202	JHA.802	,,	40
3203	JHA.803	,,	40
3204	JHA.804	,,	40
3205	JHA.805	,,	40
3206	JHA.806	,,	40
3207	JHA.807	,,	40
3208	JHA.808	,,	40
3209	JHA.809	,,	40
3210	JHA.810	,,	40
3211	JHA.811	,,	40
3212	JHA.812	,,	40

Fleet Number	Registration Number	Type and Seating		Garage Number
3213	JHA.813	"S.8"	40	
3214	JHA.814	,,	40	
3215	JHA.815	,,	40	
3216	JHA.816	,,	40	
3217	JHA.817	,,	40	
3218	JHA.818	,,	40	
3219	JHA.819	,,	40	
3220	JHA.820	,,	40	
3221	JHA.821	,,	40	
3222	JHA.822	,,	40	
3223	JHA.823	,,	40	
3224	JHA.824	,,	40	
3225	JHA.825	,,	40	
3226	JHA.826	,,	40	
3227	JHA.827	,,	40	
3228	JHA.828	,,	40	
3229	JHA.829	,,	40	
3230	JHA.830	,,	40	
3231	JHA.831	,,	40	
3232	JHA.832	,,	40	
3233	JHA.833	,,	40	
3234	JHA.834	,,	40	
3235	JHA.835	,,	40	
3236	JHA.836	,,	40	
3237	JHA.837	,,	40	
3238	JHA.838	,,	40	
3239	JHA.839	,,	40	
3240	JHA.840	,,	40	
3241	JHA.841	,,	40	
3242	JHA.842	,,	40	
3243	JHA.843	,,	40	
3244	JHA.844	,,	40	
3245	JHA.845	,,	40	
3246	JHA.846	,,	40	
3247	JHA.847	,,	40	
3248	JHA.848	,,	40	
3249	JHA.849	,,	40	
3250	JHA.850	,,	40	
3251	JHA.851	,,	40	
3252	JHA.852	,,	40	
3253	JHA.853	,,	40	
3254	JHA.854	,,	40	
3255	JHA.855	,,	40	

3256	JHA.856	"S.8"	40
3257	JHA.857	,,	40
3258	JHA.858	,,	40
3259	JHA.859	,,	40
3260	JHA.860	,,	40
3261	JHA.861	,,	40
3262	JHA.862	,,	40
3263	JHA.863	,,	40
3264	JHA.864	,,	40
3265	JHA.865	,,	40
3266	JHA.866	,,	40
3267	JHA.867	,,	40
3268	JHA.868	,,	40
3269	JHA.869	,,	40
3270	JHA.870	,,	40
3271	JHA.871	,,	40
3272	JHA.872	,,	40
3273	JHA.873	,,	40
3274	JHA.874	,,	40
3275	JHA.875	,,	40
3276	JHA.876	,,	40
3277	JHA.877	,,	40
3278	JHA.878	,,	40
3279	JHA.879	,,	40
3280	JHA.880	,,	40
3281	JHA.881	,,	40
3282	JHA.882	,,	40
3283	JHA.883	,,	40
3284	JHA.884	,,	40
3285	JHA.885	,,	40
3286	JHA.886	,,	40
3287	JHA.887	,,	40
3288	JHA.888	,,	40
3289	JHA.889	,,	40
3290	JHA.890	,,	40
3291	JHA.891	,,	40
3292	JHA.892	,,	40
3293	JHA.893	,,	40
3294	JHA.894	,,	40
3295	JHA.895	,,	40
3296	JHA.896	,,	40
3297	JHA.897	,,	40
3298	JHA.898	,,	40
3299	JHA.899	,,	40
3300	KHA.300	"C.1"	30
3301	KHA.301	,,	30

Fleet Number	Registration Number	Type and Seating		Garage Number
3302	KHA.302	"C.1"	30	
3303	KHA.303	,,	30	
3304	KHA.304	,,	30	
3305	KHA.305	,,	30	
3306	KHA.306	,,	30	
3307	KHA.307	,,	30	
3308	KHA.308	,,	30	
3309	KHA.309	,,	30	
3310	KHA.310	,,	30	
3311	KHA.311	,,	30	
3312	KHA.312	,,	30	
3313	KHA.313	,,	30	
3314	KHA.314	,,	30	
3315	KHA.315	,,	30	
3316	KHA.316	,,	30	
3317	KHA.317	,,	30	
3318	KHA.318	,,	30	
3319	KHA.319	,,	30	
3320	KHA.320	,,	30	
3321	KHA.321	,,	30	
3322	KHA.322	,,	30	
3323	KHA.323	,,	30	
3324	KHA.324	,,	30	
3325	KHA.325	,,	30	
3326	KHA.326	,,	30	
3327	KHA.327	,,	30	
3328	KHA.328	,,	30	
3329	KHA.329	,,	30	
3330	KHA.330	,,	30	
3331	KHA.331	,,	30	
3332	KHA.332	,,	30	
3333	KHA.333	,,	30	
3334	KHA.334	,,	30	
3335	KHA.335	,,	30	
3336	KHA.336	,,	30	
3337	KHA.337	,,	30	
3338	KHA.338	,,	30	
3339	KHA.339	,,	30	
3340	KHA.340	,,	30	
3341	KHA.341	,,	30	
3342	KHA.342	,,	30	
3343	KHA.343	,,	30	
3344	KHA.344	,,	30	

VEHICLE DATA

Type	Year(s) Produced	Seating Capacity	Bodywork by	Engine		Number originally produced of each type	Remarks
				Cyls. No.	P. or O. (Petrol or Oil)		
"QL"	1928	35	Brush Ransomes	4	P	170	
"M"	1929	34	Brush Ransomes	4	P	49	
"MM"	1930	34	Ransomes	6	P	60	
"IM-4"	1929-1933	34	Short Bros. Brush	4	P	169	
"IM-6"	1931-1932	34	B.M.M.O. Short Bros.	6	P	50	
"BRR"	1933	34	Short Bros.	6	P	20	
"REDD"	1932	55	Short Bros Brush Metro. Cammell Eastern Counties	6	P	50	
"FEDD"	1934-1936	56	Short Bros. Metro. Cammell	6	P	135	
"FEDD"	1937-1939	56	Brush	6	O	200	
"LRR"	1934-1935	34	Short Bros.	6	P	31	Saloon Coach, now used as service bus.

TYPE	Year(s) Produced	Seating Capacity	Bodywork	Engine		Number originally produced of each type	Remarks
				Cyls. No.	P. or O. (Petrol or Oil)		
" ON "	1935	38	Short Bros.	6	P	83	44 later converted to " CON " type.
" CON "	1934-1935	38	Short Bros.	6	O	44	" ON " type converted to Oil Engine.
" DON "	1935	36	Short Bros. Brush	6	O	49	Similar to " ON " but fitted with Oil (Diesel) Engine.
" SON "	1936-1939	38	English Electric Brush	6	O	303	
" SLR "	1937	30	English Electric	6	P	50	Saloon Coach
" OLR "	1935	34	Short Bros.	6	P	25	Originally built as Touring Coach ; converted to service bus 1942.
" ONC "	1939	30	Duple	6	O	25	Saloon Coach.
" S.6. "	1946	40	Brush Metro. Cammell	6	O	100	In production. Underfloor engine.
" A.D. 2 "	1946	56	Brush Metro. Cammell	6	O	100	In production. Mounted on A.E.C. chassis.

NOTES : This list includes only those vehicles in operation at the date of publication.
Vehicles of standard makes (e.g., Daimler, Guy, etc.), acquired during the war period have been omitted.
This list does not include a small batch of vehicles of a type known as " COD " acquired from an Associated Company during the war period.
The seating capacities shown are those of the majority of the vehicles of each type. Certain experimental vehicles exist where the seating capacity (and other details) vary from the bulk of that particular type.

MIDLAND "RED" TOURING COACHES

1925. "SOS" type open charabanc

1927-8. "QLC" type touring coach

MIDLAND "RED" TOURING COACHES

1937. "SLR" type 30-seater touring coach

1939. "ONC" type luxury touring coach